Cyber Warfare

History, Key Players, Attacks, Trends, and Keeping Yourself Safe in the Cyber Age

FERNANDO UILHERME BARBOSA DE AZEVEDO

Index

About the Author

Fernando Uilherme Barbosa de Azevedo is an electronic, electrical and industrial engineer graduated from Pontifícia Universidade Católica of Rio de Janeiro. He is MBA graduate from Fundação Getúlio Vargas. He has been a programming instructor at Pontifícia Universidade Católica of Rio de Janeiro for 7 years.

He published his first book "Macros for Excel hands on" by publisher Campus/Elsevier at age 27. The book is still sold in Brazil and Portugal.

His first startup business won a prize from the Brazilian Federal Institutional FINEP.

Coming to the United States in 2014, Fernando studied Web Development and Internet Technologies at University of California Santa Cruz - Silicon Valley Extension and also completed the "Innovation and Entrepreneurship Certification" from Stanford University.

Fernando has been featured many times in news media and TV. He was interviewed as a specialist on his field by Forbes, The Entrepreneur, el Nuevo Herald and many other major Brazilian media companies.

Today, Fernando runs 2 internet marketing companies in the United States and has clients in many countries. The companies offer services such as internet marketing, SEO, Online Reputation Managements, pen testing, systems audit, e-commerce, apps and other internet related activities.

He is also a web development instructor for IronHack and weekly speaker at Radio Gazeta.

Fernando considers himself an ethical hacker and thinks that the internet should be a safer place. By advocating against all the unethical activities online that are still present today, he hopes that our leaders and law makers can become aware of these threats and help create laws for a safer world.

This book is dedicated to Fernando's sister Christiane Monnerat.

This book is a series of 6 books related to Internet Technologies and how the internet works. If you like this book, please check out other books from the same author.

Introduction

When people talk about war and warfare the things that we all imagine about it are no less than horrific. We are often reminded of the previous two World Wars as well as other wars that remind us of how cruel man can be to his fellowman.

That is why when people bring up the subject of cyber warfare the same horrid images haunt the people. But of course where cyber warfare is concerned people imagine a world that is devoid of technology or even at least economies being destroyed by invading hackers.

But what is cyber warfare?

The interesting thing is that there is actually no singular definition of cyber warfare that fits all proposed scenarios. There are several definitions that have been put forward and they all have valid points.

Nevertheless, it should be emphasized that there is no single definition that has been accepted internationally. The former national coordinator for the Security, Infrastructure Protection and Counter-terrorism Richard Clarke once said that cyber warfare refers to the actions of one country to attack or invade another nation's computers or computer network.

That is of course a very broad definition and is very open to discussion. Another very open definition is that it is a series or an entire campaign of cyber-attacks that is conducted by one entity on another entity.

That means one company or business can conduct cyber warfare on another company or business. Some may argue that any cyber-attack can then be labelled as cyber warfare if that will be the definition that we will adopt.

Those who have a penchant for military constructs on the other hand believe that cyber warfare is only such if the cyber-attacks take on a military-like level. That means the hacks and other network attacks target military infrastructures and systems. That would include attacks on weapon design facilities, army bases, and the other military assets of a country.

However, not all attacks committed in cyber warfare will and have targeted military infrastructures. Some have been aimed at financial institutions, other essential resources of a country, and even private businesses such as hotels, airlines, casinos, and financial institutions like banks and other similar businesses. In fact, small businesses that have less than 500 employees are also targets of hackers and other cyber groups.

Some cyber-attacks are conducted by entities that are officially sponsored by a country's government. On the other hand some attacks are conducted by groups that aren't tied or sponsored by any actual government branch or agency.

These groups act on their own accord and do it for their own ideals and goals. However, do take note that cyber groups will need huge amounts of resources to engage in full scale cyber warfare—something that governments around the world should be able to provide.

Some cyber warfare attacks are conducted by terrorists while others are done by ideological groups. There are also attacks that were committed by criminal organizations that of course benefit them entirely and not necessarily contribute to a country's welfare or advantage.

Part of cyber warfare is of course the defense of a country's network infrastructure. So it is not just hackers fighting alongside military forces such as some may have envisioned it, but it also involves the defense created to prevent offensives from those outside a nation. They prevent infiltration by foreign hackers or they strike back at them, whichever is the case.

In this book we will cover both sides—attacks and defense. We will cover the different cyber-attacks that have been and can be used and the motives behind such actions.

It is also important to know and understand the different parties that are involved in cyber warfare. Most cyber groups today may have already been disbanded or reorganized. We will cover the cyber-attacks that have been performed or suspected to have been performed and the amount of damage that was done.

Another important question that will be addressed is how we can protect our own information and data from such attacks. We know that there is no realistic way to make sure that our computer systems can become 100% impregnable.

There will always be loopholes in our computer infrastructure. Even though how safe you think your computer is there will always be a way for anyone to break into your system and take advantage of the information contained in it. Anyone can vouch for that—ask any cyber security expert, and he will confess to such a truth. However, there ways to prevent attacks and at least keep your data and information as safe as you can make it.

But make no mistake about it.

We are already at war.

Cyber warfare is a controversial subject and you won't find a lot of hard evidence to point at the offending party. One thing is for sure, if any party is engaged in cyber warfare—whether they are defending or attacking—you can be sure that those who are at the frontline of cyber defense can also take the offensive and commit the same atrocious attacks that they were trying to thwart.

We'll go over all of these issues and more as we go along.

Thanks for buying this book, I hope you enjoy it!

Chapter 1: The Secret History of Cyber Warfare

Have you seen the movie The Fight Club? What is the first rule of Fight Club? It's all about secrecy. The reason why the system was so effective was that it was so secretive. The same rule applies to cyber warfare. It is a type of warfare that is enveloped and laced in secrecy.

In this chapter we will attempt to trace the history of cyber history—yes, we can only attempt to do so. You can't dig into its very roots and insides because the first rule is...

Well, you should know the answer to that question.

New Combat Domains

The latest information and security training is fast becoming a necessity as the world becomes more aware of the cyber warfare that has been going on for decades. History is a hard teacher. Unfortunately we may need to learn from its lessons since learning from the past is paramount in preparation for the future.

National Defense University's Dan Kuehl (Washington D.C.) says that other than the old war domains of air, land, and sea, today's warfare is fought on two new zones—cyberspace and outer space. Wars are now fought with a keyboard on a computer as it is with guns, aircraft, or weapons of mass destruction.

Three Cyber Warfare Methods

Security experts have identified three main methods of warfare in cyberspace. They are: electronic espionage, sabotage, and attacks on essential public service installations such as power grids etc.

The NERC or North American Electric Reliability Corporation has at one time issues a public warning that the electrical grid in the United States is susceptible to attack. The computer infrastructure that is used by public services such as gas, power, hospital services, emergency services, and others still make use of older technology. That is technology that can be hacked and controlled remotely.

Russian mafia group RBN or Russian Business Network launched an intensive identity theft campaign back in 2006. They used a tool that they developed which is known as Storm Worm—a virus/worm that gathers information computer systems.

A year later it is estimated that there were around 1 million computers infected by Storm Worm and they send infected emails daily. The infection was so widespread that the very computers in the Pentagon were allegedly hacked.

Personal computers weren't the only computer units that were affected by these attacks. Even computers from government institutions and departments were also victimized by identity theft attacks. In August 27, 2008, NASA confirmed that even the computers in the International Space Station were hacked. It is alleged that it was the Russians who conducted these attacks.

Private companies are also vulnerable to these cyber-attacks. For example, back in December 254, 2008, India's largest bank The State Bank of India was attacked by Pakistani hackers. Even though no data was reported to be lost, the attack forced the bank to shut down their website, which meant that customers didn't have access to their funds for at least one day.

Of the three methods of attack, espionage is somewhat the least worrisome come to think about it. But sabotage and the disruption of public services is seen as the most destructive attack. You can already imagine hackers shutting down the entire power grid or causing factories to crash. The havoc that these kinds of attacks can cause is no less than catastrophic.

Fred Kaplan's "Dark Territory: The Secret History of Cyber War"

Fred Kaplan is a journalist and an author. He writes a weekly column for Slate magazine entitled War Stories. Kaplan usually covers the US foreign policy and international relations.

One of the books he wrote is Dark Territory: The Secret History of Cyber War. This book undertook the role of filling the gaps in cyber war history or at least give its readers a behind the scenes glimpse of the events that took place.

Of course we can't expect the book to cover everything about the history of cyber war. However, he does include a lot of nuggets that help shed light on a lot of things. For instance, he shows in his book that early on in the history of the development of the internet that the vulnerability of shared networks has been discovered or at least identified as early as 1967.

It was Willis Howard Ware who brought up the issue as early as the late 1960s in his paper, entitled *Security and Privacy in Computer Systems.* It was a 32 page document and was presented at the Spring Joint Computer Conference in Atlantic City back in April 17, 1967. That actually lays down the point that Kaplan was making – and that is none of the cyber security issues that we are facing are really new. These issues are actually decades old. In fact, Kaplan says that it can be traced from the very beginning of the internet.

You see when Willis Ware pointed out that seemingly obvious flaw no one listened to him. What Ware was saying essentially is that when you open a connection to your computer here and allow another computer remote access then you have opened a gateway for that computer to access yours. This is essentially the problem when you put information on a network. You have already created an inherent vulnerability.

In short, what Willis Ware was saying is that you are not going to be able to keep secrets anymore. So what happened since the day Ware pointed out the flaws in computer networks? What happened was that entire networks have been developed all over the world decades later without even a single provision for security. You can say that this weakness in the internet infrastructure was embedded in the technology itself.

So what does all of this imply?

What this means is that cyber security problems will actually never go away. You can't control it, you can't mitigate it, and you can also contain it, but you can never solve it. How can we say this? Well, just read what Willis Ware wrote more than 30 years back—what he describes in that paper is still the same issues that are being discussed today.

Sure our technology has grown and developed at astounding proportions but its inherent weakness is still there. Why didn't people listen to Ware back then? Kaplan points out that back then not a lot of people had computers at home.

The majority of people were not concerned because they were not greatly impacted by it at the time. The people in the NSA and others who took part in the development of internet technology said that Russia wouldn't be able to do the same things that they were doing decades since. But that changed through the decades and somehow everyone forgot about the issues that Ware raised or they just conveniently pushed them to the sidelines.

Ronald Reagan and NSDD 145

The very first actual and serious response to the security issues raised by Willis Ware happened in 1984 via the National Security Decision Directive 145 . NSDD 145 is the first presidential directive that centered on computer security. Again this document is also available for public viewing.

This directive was signed by then US president Ronald Reagan back in September 17, 1984. It provided an organizational structure, essential policies, and initial objectives for providing protection for computer systems and related assets.

It basically put the NSA (National Security Agency), DoD (Department of Defense), and the NSC (National Security Council) at the forefront of protecting the nation's sensitive information.

These organizations and branches of government were to be responsible for the development of technical standards, determining the vulnerabilities of computer systems, and safeguarding information. Furthermore, the NSA was directed to develop safeguards for sensitive information.

The funny thing is that NSDD 145 only came about because President Ronald Reagan was watching a movie Wargames, which was shown the year before in 1983. The premise or plot of the movie was that a teenage hacker was able to gain access to NORAD's defense systems and almost triggered World War III.

When Reagan gathered his staff the following day for a security meeting he brings out the topic but everyone was oblivious. But he tasked one of his generals to look into it. A week later the general reports to him and said that the situation was much worse. And so a year later NSDD 145 was released.

In Kaplan's book the early narrative was not of hackers breaking into networks and defenders trying to keep them out. A lot of the situations he reports were of bureaucrats warring with each other with each one serving their own interests.

Note that even though Kaplan doesn't mention all his sources, it would appear that a lot of them were senior policy makers. You know, the ones who made decisions that could have swayed things one way or the other. These turf battles early in the history of cyber warfare has a lasting impact and we are now feeling it today.

NSDD 145 may have increased the awareness of policy makers when it was released but it wasn't enough to cause greater public awareness. Back in the 80s you don't have nearly as much computer exposure as we do today.

Some of the policies that were later released defined and also limited what information the government can release to the public. For instance, the NSC released a policy statement in October of 1986 that restricted access to sensitive information.

This and other restrictions made by the government were met with a lot of concern from the public. These efforts were met with resistance and of course protests from the business community, civil liberties organizations, and groups from the scientific community. Congressional hearings were later conducted and even NSDD 145 was placed under review.

By the year 1990 NSDD 145 was replaced in 1990 by a National Security Directive which is NSD 42 to be precise. There were other security directives that were released as well such as Homeland Security Presidential Directive 24.

Cyber Warfare: Brief Historic Timeline

- 2010

The launch of Stuxnet: Stuxnet was released: Well it was more like discovered but it seems that it was developed several years earlier. Stuxnet was the very first genuine cyber weapon. Yes, this is not just your run of the mill malware or virus or spyware. Stuxnet was designed to cause physical damage—an actual weapon that uses cyber technology. Reports say that Sutxnet destroyed about a fifth of the nuclear centrifuges of Iran.

- 2014

March 2014—DDoS attack on Ukraine: Russia is known for launching combined cyber and military attacks. Now, these are coordinated attacks with cyber groups working behind the technical side to aid military efforts. The DDoS (Distributed Denial of Service) attack they launched against Ukraine in 2014 was 32 times larger than any such attacks that were ever recorded.

The result was that the entire internet in Ukraine was disrupted. That meant no one had access to internet service. This of course crippled telecoms and other means of communication as well as public service. This DDoS attack went on while Crimea was being seized by pro-Russian rebels.

May 2014—Disruption of Ukrainian Elections: Russia was again at it but this time there was no coordinated attacks. A hacker group that was known to be Russian based was on the job days before Ukraine's presidential election. They hacked into the country's election commission and one of their backup systems. This was an attempt to create chaos and of course there was a pro-Russian candidate who was running for office during that electoral campaign.

- 2015

June 2015—Germany vs. Russia: Russia is known to be quite active when it comes to cyber-attacks but they're not alone. There are other countries that are actively engaged in cyber warfare. We'll go over each one of them later.

In June 2015 the German Bundestag network was hacked by Russian operatives, this according to the BfV (i.e. the country's intelligence service). German investigators said that the Russians were looking for information on NATO, German leaders, and the Bundestag as well

June 2015—China vs. United States: The Office of Personnel Management of the United States was attacked by Chinese cyber operatives and they stole 21.5 million employee records including failed applicants' information.

December 2015—Western Ukraine Power Outage: Russian cyber operatives hacked into Ukraine's power grid system. They then proceeded to cut off power to western Ukraine. That meant that around 225,000 people didn't have electric power for a time.

- 2016

December 2016—Ukraine Power Outage: Russia was at it again and caused another power outage in Ukraine. We can guess that they are trying to prove something. To think that Ukraine officials and their departments could have done something to plug any cyber leaks in their system we can say that Russian cyber groups were trying to say that Ukraine's side of the table couldn't do anything.

What the Russians did actually was to implant their bugs in the supplier's network. They kept their cyber weapons there lying dormant and undetected. They waited a total of six months before launching another cyber-attack that caused another widespread power outage. The attack was launched at night and 1/5 of Kiev's power went offline.

- 2017

May 2017—WannaCry: WannaCry is another cyber weapon and it was launched in 2017. It is actually a type of ransomware and cryptoworm (more info on that in the next chapter) and it targets computers that ran Windows operating systems. It is estimated that this cryptoworm spread to more than 150 countries around the world and it infected more than 200,000 computers. Note that this is just one ransomware released into the internet but it was not yet weaonized.

June 2017—NotPetya: NotPetya is another type of ransomware just like WannaCry. But the big difference is that NotPetya is weaponized. In other words it is just not another virus—it's an actual cyber weapon.

NotPetya was actually disguised as a type of ransomware when it fact it wasn't just locking up people's computers, which is what ransomware usually do. NotPetya was a weapon, it actually destroyed computer files.

The attack, as investigators found out, originated from Ukraine—the country where this cyber weapon was unleashed. However, it quickly spread all over the world. Authorities estimate that the damage it caused cost more than 10 billion dollars.

An Unprecedented Risk

Cyber warfare is nothing short of an unprecedented risk. Even though the major cyber groups sponsored by different countries attack focus their attacks on important infrastructures and installations such as hospitals, banks, power grids, and transport systems, we should not remain complacent.

Cyber-attacks can come from abroad and the scary part is that it can also come from home. There are local individuals and other hackers that come from your own home country as well.

Some of them are the brilliant minds in the internet and computer industry. Well, think about it—when you know how to protect a computer system from viruses, worms, malware, and other hacks it also means you understand how these malicious computer programs work. In other words you can create one of your own too.

Cyber-attacks are considered criminal acts today. And that is what we will go over in the next chapter. We will go over some of the top threats considered by the authorities and go over some of the tips that will help protect you from them.

Chapter 2: Crimes in the Name of Warfare

In the United States, the FBI is the leading organization or federal agency that is tasked with investigating and preventing cyber-attacks by criminals. Criminals in cyber space include entities, groups, and individuals within the country's territory as well as overseas. They are also tasked with combatting and apprehending terrorists as well as cyber terrorists.

The Threat is Real

Cyber threats are real.

Believe it or not but the FBI considers the threat of cyber warfare as real as it can get. In fact the organization considers it as an incredibly serious threat to the nation's security. Not only is this a current threat among us today but this threat is also continually growing—which is perhaps part of the reason why it is so scary.

Cyber intrusions according to the FBI are becoming more sophisticated as the years go by. That means these threats are becoming more dangerous and definitely more commonplace.

We used to think that if you do not have a significant amount of money or influence then cyber criminals and cyber terrorists will leave you alone. What's a couple of thousand dollars in your bank account compared to the millions in a federal bank, right?

It's easier to keep an eye on accounts that have smaller amounts of money that the accounts of big corporations that holds millions if not billions. It would be ideal to attack those accounts since no one would notice several hundred thousands of it missing. Well, by the time they did find out eventually that money was stolen the perpetrator of such a cyber-attack will have been long gone.

But guess what. That is no longer true in the 21st century.

The FBI sees the country's internet infrastructure as something that is critically exposed. That is the entire nation and not just big businesses and government facilities. That is everyone both in the public and private sectors.

Cyber criminals attack American companies big or small not for just the funds that they may be able to steal. It's not just all about the money anymore nowadays. In many instances, companies in the US are attacked to obtain their trade secrets.

If not the trade secrets of that company, the perpetrators are after sensitive corporate data. That also includes the private information of employees, staff, and leaders of an organization.

Universities have also become targets of these cyber-attacks as well. So, what do cyber terrorists and cyber criminals want with student and faculty information? Well, it's not exactly their personal or bank info that they're after. Note that there are universities and educational institutions that literally spearhead the next cutting edge technologies. That is exactly what cyber-attacks are targeting—the most advanced research and development.

But those are large institutions—they shouldn't affect private individuals, right? Well, no. Identity theft has become rampant here and there. The goal of course is to commit fraud. A darker part of cyber-crime targets children, which are particular interests of online predators.

Since the 9/11 terror attacks, the FBI has gone through a rapid transformation. We can say that they are better equipped today to address future cyber-attacks and are better able to gather intel on other possible terrorist threats.

Today they are undergoing another kind of transformation—
they are trying to address the ever changing and rapidly
evolving threat of cyber warfare. They have formed their Cyber
Division and that team is currently being enhanced so that
they can better address intrusions into private and
government computer networks.

What are the FBI's Priorities in Cyber Warfare?

Of course the FBI will prioritize certain types of cyber-crimes
over others. Identity theft is high on the list since it is quite
prevalent nowadays. The organization is also on an intensive
hunt for online predators. However, at the top of the list
priority cases are network and computer intrusions and
ransomware as well. Let's look at these priority cases.

Identity Theft

Identity theft refers to the illegal acquisition and use of
another person's personal and private identifying information
(e.g. social number etc.). The goal behind such fraudulent acts
is usually financial gain.

The FBI has stated that identity theft has become increasingly
facilitated due to better, more efficient, and faster internet
technology. Again, the main goal behind identity theft is either
fraud or theft. The FBI also incorporates its intelligence assets
to resolve identity theft cases.

Online Predators

This is probably one of the most serious online threats that the
FBI is monitoring. It should also be one of the biggest

concerns of families everywhere especially if your children are active on the internet.

The FBI sponsors the Violent Crimes Against Children Program which is managed by the agency's Criminal Investigative Division. That means there are two departments that are directly engaged and are cooperating in this effort. Their teams investigate peer to peer file sharing programs and networks, online forums, bulletin board systems, relay chat channels, internet news groups, websites that post child pornography, social networking sites, and other related online services.

Network and Computer Intrusions

These cyber-attacks include any form of illegal or unauthorized access to computers and the networks that these systems are connected to. The FBI reports that the sheer impact of the total number of intrusions each year is actually quite staggering.

They report that the country loses billions of dollars each year due to these unwarranted intrusions. The cost of repairing these attacks alone is already a huge cost to businesses and individuals who fall victims to hackers.

Some attacks can sometimes disrupt the services of hospitals, public service agencies (e.g. 911), and even financial institutions like banks. It's not just a disruption of these basic services, sometimes what happens is that the operations of these businesses and organizations get disabled.

Now, the next question is who are the perpetrators of these illegal intrusions?

Some may think that the people responsible for illegal intrusions into the networks and computers of government agencies and businesses come from abroad. However, the FBI reports that the huge portion of the number of attacks come from within the country.

That includes computer geeks who try their knack at hacking just to get some sort of bragging rights. It's their way of showing off their skills to their community of geeks and hackers.

Another huge source of these illegal intrusions comes from competitor businesses as well. They hack into competitor websites and other cyber properties searching for trade secrets and other means to get the upper hand in their respective markets.

Yet another significant source, it could be more commonplace than the two previous sources of illegal network and computer intrusions, rings of criminals. Their goal is to steal relevant customer, personal, and financial or baking information from pretty much anyone and anywhere. Why steal that information? They sell to black markets where the said information is absolutely valued.

If that wasn't enough, the FBI is also tasked with monitoring and countering the activities of terrorists and spies who are always looking for ways to either launch cyber strikes or steal sensitive information. These latter groups actually pose the biggest threats to national security—but that doesn't mean they won't perform cyber strikes on the general public.

The FBI's operations to counter computer and network intrusions include the following:

- The FBI created a Cyber Division right in their headquarters. This division is responsible for addressing all forms of cyber-crimes using cohesive and coordinated efforts.

- The agency is currently collaborating with other government agencies that also share similar concerns. They work closely with the Department of Homeland Security as well as the Department of Defense.

- Cyber Action Teams have also been formed. These teams travel all over the world to gather data and intelligence as well as to assist in the efforts to of other cooperating foreign governments and their agencies. These teams handle those cases that pose the biggest threats to the national economy and national security. They often go after the most dangerous personalities and groups on the FBI's hit list.

- The FBI headquarters and all of their field offices all over the country have cyber squads as part of their regular staff. They are tasked with investigating online fraud, child exploitation and pornography, and the theft of personal and intellectual property.

The Threat of Ransomware

Large businesses, law enforcement agencies, local governments, schools, and even hospitals are some of the usual victims of ransomware. Ransomware refers to any kind of malware that locks and encrypts valuable files on computer systems.

A ransom is then demanded for the release of these valuable files.

The basic idea is pretty much the same as holding someone for ransom. The damage however can be catastrophic considering the loss of proprietary and sensitive information.

The regular operations of businesses can be disrupted. Sometimes this attack can cost a company some considerable amount of financial losses. At times it can cost the reputation of an organization.

Home computers are also susceptible. Even though the losses incurred by regular folks aren't as much as those incurred by large businesses and government agencies, these people lose valuable data and information nonetheless. Personal videos, photos, online certificates, personal records, and other information is still valuable to those who own them.

How Does a Ransomware Attack Happen?

One of the common ways that ransomware get into a computer is either through email or some innocent looking link or URL on the web. Emails will be addressed to individuals and they will seem legit enough.

Yes, they can be quite convincing and so these people click it or when they click on an attachment in that email then the ransomware gets downloaded to the computer's local hard drive.

The email may contain an electronic fax or maybe an invoice and yes it will look like the stuff that gets circulated in your office. The same is true when you find a URL or link that looks innocent or legit. You click on that and the browser redirects you to a different site. All the while ransomware code is already infecting your computer.

Once ransomware has infected a computer it will begin to encrypt files and folders in the hard drive. Any backup drive or flash drive that you connect can also be potentially infected.

And that is also how ransomware gets spread throughout the office or from one computer to the other in your home. Most of the time computer users are generally not aware that their systems have already been infected by ransomware.

The only time they become aware of the attack is when they can't access their files. When that happens they will also get messages demanding a payment in exchange for a decryption key (i.e. access to your own files). The instructions will include the method you should use to pay the expected ransom. Most of the time, the payment comes in the form of Bitcoin or some other form of cryptocurrency.

Ransomware nowadays have become more sophisticated. There are types of them that no longer need emails or even the need for a computer user to click a link or go to a particular website—phishing sites included. Legitimate sites nowadays can be seeded with malicious code that attack software that is unpatched or systems that lack the necessary protection updates.

How to Handle Ransomware

The FBI does not recommend that you pay the ransom demanded of you if ever you do become a victim of a ransomware attack. Even if you do pay the ransom it will not guarantee that you will be given back your access to your data.

There have been many times when people and organizations have paid the ransom and still were not given any decryption keys. Paying ransoms also emboldens criminals and the will tend to target more people and organizations. It means you end up giving them more incentives to continue in this illegal activity.

So, what is the FBI's advice with regard to ransomware? People should focus on preventive efforts. That means you should train your employees how to avoid such threats. A company's computer system and network should also be updated with the latest preventive tools and controls.

You should also create a business continuity plan in the event of the loss of data. That means you should treat getting a ransomware attack the equivalent of losing your data due to a virus or computer equipment breakdown. That would entail the creation of data backups that you can access so you can recover from any losses incurred.

Here are some tips from the FBI:

- Create secure backups

- Backups should not be connected to the computer systems that hold the original data

- Backups should be made regularly and their integrity should be verified as well

- Implement software restrictions (no one should install unauthorized software in any computer in your company)

- You should also have protective software as well as network permissions at different levels

- Install controls that prevent programs from running in the usual areas where ransomware start to execute such as compression/decompression programs, certain internet browsers, and temporary folders.

- Disable macro scripts in office files and documents especially those that are transmitted through email.

- Configure access controls to different sections of the network

- You should only share network permissions appropriately

- The use of privileged account should be carefully managed

- Set anti-malware as well as anti-virus tools to update regularly and automatically

- Always patch your operating systems, digital devices, and firmware as needed

The FBI's Tips on How to Protect Your Computer

The following are the tips that you can find on the FBI's website on how to protect your computer from cyber-attacks. This is only a short list of tips and they will not be as detailed. We will cover cyber protection techniques and best practices in a separate chapter of this book.

- *Turn off your computer* – sometimes it's great to have your computer turned on 24/7 and ready for any task that you need to do. But since our internet connections are set to "always on" that leaves an opening for anyone to hack your device. Turning off your computer means keeping it disconnected, which helps to prevent a lot of different cyber-attacks—you can't do cyber-attacks on a device that is off the grid.

- *Be careful of the things you download* – don't just download any email attachment. Be wary of emails from people you don't know and emails that were just forwarded to you.

- *Update your operating system* – operating systems are updated by their manufacturers periodically. Some are security updates and some updates are critical in nature. You don't really need to download every single update that comes up but when security and critical updates come up, make sure that your OS will alert you when such things happen.

- *Install and update your antispyware and antivirus software* – spyware and viruses can wreak havoc on any computer system. The best way to deal with them is by installing software that can detect them and remove them from your system.

- *Keep your firewall up* – firewalls are your first line of defense from hackers. Sure some hackers may find a way to break through firewalls but they act as deterrents that can discourage a hacker since it will make things more difficult for them.

It should be noted that the FBI is not the only government agency that is working to stop cybercrime and monitor the activities of actors and elements that are involved in cyber warfare. The NSA and also the DoD are at the frontlines and they also consider cyber as a primary threat in our highly connected world.

Chapter 3: At the Top of the DoD's Threat List

Cyber warfare and cyber-attacks and threats are part of our reality today. In fact, these threats are considered the biggest threat according to the Director of National Intelligence. This is according to a 2018 report by the US Department of Defense.

So, why did it make it to the very top of the list of threats to national security? One of the reasons cited in that report by the DOD is the rapid growth of cyber technology. The faster is its growth the bigger the threat.

America's vulnerability to cyber threats is also growing as the country becomes more and more dependent on that technology. In fact, it is not only a threat the United States---it is in fact a threat to all nations of the world.

Daniel Coats, the fifth Director of National Intelligence reported to a Senate Select Committee on Intelligence. There he covered what he and the intelligence committee as the biggest threats to the US.

Some of the entities and threats that he mentioned in that meeting included terrorism in general, North Korea, China, and also Russia. However, he did not lead the discussion with those four major threats. He actually started with cyber war and it was at the top of his list.

A Multifaceted and Complex Enemy

When you think of cyber warfare you sometimes form the picture in your head of some kind of technological arms race against other countries. It is as if you are in an actual battleground where the field of battle is the internet.

You can almost imagine everyone in a frantic hurry to outdo the other hackers and programmers of the opposing countries. It is some kind of secret war since everything and every confrontation is covert. Well, think of it as some sort of an open secret where everyone knows but you act like you don't know a thing. And the funny thing is that everyone acts as if they don't know that you know what they are doing in the background.

It's not exactly like that but in some ways it is. Coats said that the cyber threat is both challenging and complex. Sure there are other countries with elite cyber groups under their command. But apart from government backed cyber organizations, there are also individuals as well as non-affiliated groups who participate in cyber warfare as well.

Again, as it was explained elsewhere in this book, the motives behind cyber-attacks aren't always political or ideological. Sometimes individuals and cyber groups do it just for bragging rights.

Where Do the Threats Come From?

Daniel Coats mentioned several countries and other places where people trained or knowledgeable in cyber warfare could come from in his report. The term he used was "actors" which could refer to single individuals or to groups that are coordinated in their efforts.

They make use of cyber technology along with other tools to create international hotspots, force changes in international rules, shape societies, also to move institutions into action or positions. These changes will be to the advantage of cyber warfare groups or the actors that Coats was referring to.

He also mentioned other possible threats like Latin America, Asia, Middle East, and Africa. Although some of these actors are not directly using cyber as a way to attack the United States, their objectives fall into the category of committing violence and causing instability within and among the states as well.

The Race for Technological Superiority

As it was mentioned in other parts of this book, there is a race for technological superiority that is ongoing and the US is part of that race. As countries mount and develop their defenses and cyber tools, some of threats will also try to sow division within countries and weaken its leadership.

That will of course add to their cyber advantage. If government agencies are too busy fighting among themselves then that gives these actors time to work on their strategies and cyber warfare tools.

Coats mentioned that North Korea, Iran, Russia, and China pose the greatest threats as far as cyber warfare is concerned. He specifically mentions Russia as using cyber-attacks not only to attack the US directly but also to weaken the country's alliances. The target of course is not only the US but also other European countries that are allied with the USA.

There are Other Cyber Threats

It will be interesting to note that direct cyber-attacks are not the only threats of this type that countries around the world will have to watch out for. He mentioned that China uses its cyber capabilities for espionage. The goal of their country's cyber unit may not be to spread terror but to penetrate networks of other countries in support of their country's national security and its economic policies.

Just like China, Iran also uses cyber warfare for espionage. However, part of their efforts is to help to lay down the necessary groundwork for future network incursions.

North Korea on the other hand gathers intelligence through cyber efforts not only to launch attacks against other countries (that includes South Korea and the US). Part of their cyber efforts includes being able to raise funds and intelligence gathering.

It's Not Just Cyber Threats

After cyber threats, weapons of mass destruction or WMDs are on spot number 2 of the biggest threats to the United States. There are countries that have undergoing efforts to acquire WMDs. But that is not the only thing that they need. They also need to acquire a delivery system for these weapons as well as the underlying technologies to properly use them.

North Korea was cited as one of the biggest potential threats. Coats labeled the country as the most confrontational threat. He also revealed that the country also has ongoing biological and chemical warfare programs apart from ballistic missiles and a growing number of nuclear warheads.

It's not just North Korea, other countries like China and Russia are also working to improve and grow their arsenals— that means that they already have WMDs too. Pakistan on the other hand also has efforts to develop nuclear weaponry. However, theirs is more short range arms than anything that can directly affect countries far away.

Chemical weapons have also been used by Syria but that is in response to the civil war they are experiencing in their country. The countries that are posturing in these efforts will love to obtain WMDs and also chemical weapons. Can you combine cyber weapons and weapons of mass destruction? Other countries like Russia have performed coordinated attacks using cyber and conventional warfare. The answer is yes.

Chapter 4: Are We Ready for Cyber War?

It is a fact that history is dotted and even blighted by wars. Wars were behind the rise and fall of kingdoms and empires. Some of them are so brutal and so bloody that they are remembered even after many generations have come and gone.

Some still accuse the predecessors of the participants in that great war of some heinous crimes committed by their ancestors. However, we are only left with horrific memories and images of those dark days. Judging who is at fault with atrocities committed during those wars will be no less than a monumental task.

Today, physical battlefields are still very much the order of war. However, a new battlefield has emerged. Advanced technology has facilitated new ways to attack other nations and much of it is covert in nature.

The Rise of Cyber Warfare

Cyber-attacks have been better enabled by the advancement of technology in the 21st century. Yes, we are creating better security systems but at the same time the same technology that everyone is using can also be used to facilitate cyber-attacks. As the attacks become more sophisticated being able to find loopholes in defenses that has been setup, the defenses that we setup also make things more sophisticated. One thing leads to the other.

Needless to say, man's innovative thinking, the growing reach of the internet, and the power of our computer systems are continually transforming the way nations fight in cyber warfare.

Attack on Estonia: Early Sign of Digital Warfare Advancement

Countries with less developed cyber technologies are facing difficulties coping up with their rivals. As you will see later, this has led to countries banding together to lend support where they can. Nevertheless, a lot of countries are still left unprepared.

One example is in the 2007 cyber-attack on Estonia. The country didn't have the web infrastructure and security measures set in place to prevent or even circumvent the attacks.

The attack launched against the country was a DDoS or Distributed Denial of Service. The result of these attacks included the crash of crucial national infrastructure—i.e. their entire internet service was terribly affected or malfunctioned. Essential government services were also put to a halt due to the DDoS attack.

A Moldovan student claimed responsibility for the said attacks. However, the evidence shows that the entire operation was too big for a single person to have executed everything.

For one thing it was determined that command and control servers that were used to carry out the attacks on Estonia were traced all the way back to Russia. Furthermore, it was suspected that there were more attackers involved given the volume and level of sophistication of the attacks that were used.

It was also discovered that Russia could have stepped in as soon as the attack was discovered yet the chose not to give aid gave rise to suspicions that the Russian government was involved. In fact they also refused to cooperate with Estonia during criminal investigations. It would appear that the 2007 Estonian cyber-attacks may have been orchestrated by Russian cyber groups that were launched for Russian national interests.

But this wasn't the only cyber-attack that Russia is accused of. More recently in the previous presidential elections cyber-attacks were launched against Democratic Party groups that crippled their operations. The US accused Russian hackers who were believed to be state sponsored to be behind these attacks.

It was believed that these attacks aided in the victory of Donald Trump in the said presidential elections. Of course the spokesperson for Vladimir Putin, the Russian president, denied these accusations even calling them rubbish.

North Korean Participation

You wouldn't think that a country that is reclusive to the world around them would even think to participate in a high tech war. But things would surprise a lot of people when they learned that North Korea may also be (and is actually likely to be) playing its cards in the world of cyber warfare.

What they have is a bit of an advantage when it comes to intelligence gathering and cyber tactics. The entire country has closed off everything very well to the rest of the world. It will be a monumental task let's say to get someone into North Korea and then plug a USB stick that is equipped with a cyber weapon. On top of that, hacking into North Korea's network is already hard enough on its own.

We all know that the country is already working on its nuclear program in spite of the economic and financial difficulties that they are facing. However, you can't count them out when it comes to cyber warfare. They too have some of the most brilliant minds at their disposal—not to mention that their supreme ruler is one who is also no less than brilliant.

It is suspected that in 2015 that North Korea was responsible for a string of cyber-attacks. Yes, it hasn't been confirmed yet and the North isn't admitting anything. Allegedly, a North Korean cyber group hacked a private company—Sony Pictures Entertainment.

The personal information of the company's employees and the private information of their families have also been leaked. In response to the accusations, the country's official news agency dismissed everything as "wild rumors" and that maybe the cyber-attacks were no less than an act of support from the country's sympathizers and supporters.

Bridging the Grey Legal Area

Even regular warfare has rules – we refer to them as the rules of engagement. In the movies you will even hear some of the soldiers citing the Geneva Convention. The Geneva Convention of course includes treaties and protocols for humanitarian treatment during war times.

These protocols and treaties were established back in 1949 at the end of World War II. But the treaties weren't new only added upon after the aftermath of the holocaust. Several other protocols were added after that.

The problem with cyber warfare is that there is nothing like a Geneva Convention for it. Of course countries will call foul on the actions of others. The parties that are accused will always deny having to do with anything about the accused cyber-attacks. Remember, in this type of warfare espionage is a huge part of the game.

That means the legalities regarding the conducts of cyber warfare are in a grey area. This is why the legal status of cyber warfare is actually blurred. There are no international laws that directly and completely address the matter.

Well, obviously it is a fairly new concept anyway. However, that doesn't mean there is no international law that covers cyber warfare to some degree. There are relevant laws that cover parts of it but they are only piecemeal so to speak. The little bits and pieces of legislation that is out there are scattered and a lot of them are open to interpretation.

This grey area in the law is that thing that many countries involved in this type of digital warfare are not shy to dance around on. In fact even the ones who you thought would be on your side may be the ones who have exploited certain loopholes in them. That also gave different countries ways to test their cyber war capabilities.

But the good news is that international laws are slowly being hammered down to cover the many different aspects of cyber warfare. There are law scholars who are currently working hard to iron out the details showing how international laws can also be applied to digital war.

Their work is now the basis of what has come to be known as the Tallinn Manual. The Tallinn Manual is backed by the CCDCoE or Cooperative Cyber Defence Centre of Excellence, a NATO affiliated group. Just a bit of FYI, Tallinn is the capital of Estonia where the first known cyber-attack occurred.

The Tallinn Manual has undergone several revisions and as the conduct of cyber warfare continues we can expect that it will undergo some more changes in the future. It will also take time before it can be approved by all nations. But if it does become something akin to the Geneva Convention or better then we may see (or hope to see) cyber warfare conducted through more regulated methods.

This manual took into consideration some of the most serious and also the rarest cyber-attacks that have been committed.

The cyber-attacks that were under consideration included the ones that made use of a considerable level of force. Apart from that, the Tallinn Manual in a way established a legal framework that everyone can work with.

The goal is to establish a certain threshold. One of the questions that need to be answered is what level of cyber-attack can be considered as permissible, if it is at all possible to establish that. More over this manual is highly concerned whether a cyber-attack is in violation of international law. It also establishes certain guidelines as to how and when governments can respond to cyber assaults, which translates to the rules of engagement in cyber space.

The current version of the Tallinn Manual has a total of 154 rules, which serve as the guidelines for the conduct of cyber warfare. These rules also represent how lawyers see how international laws apply to the conduct of cyber war. Some of the rules try to protect the computers that are used in hospitals and medical institutions. Some of the rules cover the employment of cyber mercenaries.

The idea is not to prevent cyber-attacks from happening—that will happen regardless of the law being present or not. It is believed rather that if you can make the law on cyber warfare a lot clearer then that will help to prevent the escalation of attacks that can be launched. It has been observed that cyber-attacks escalate when leaders of different nations over react and the rules are not clear.

The second update or version of Tallinn Law takes into consideration the legal status of different hacks and cyber-attacks during times of peace. Note that hundreds of cyber-attacks occur each day. The additional sets of rules set forth in Tallin Law allow leaders to judge whether such attacks violate international law.

Cyber War Regulation Raises More Questions

Even though there are laws being developed that may help with the conduct of cyber warfare, it will still be too early to say whether such laws will finally resolve some of the most critical issues or not. Note that laws and regulations for this type of warfare is everyone's concerns.

In March 15, 2018 the UN Secretary General Antonio Guterres called for measures to control cyber warfare when he addressed the Human Rights Council. He actually did it in two of his speeches with the first one being in February 2018.

It has also been pointed out that cyber war was already ongoing between different states. The secretary general also admits that the world leaders haven't discussed whether such ongoing warfare can be covered under international humanitarian laws or even by the Geneva Convention. Currently it isn't clear whether such treaties and regulations apply to cyber warfare.

However, this call for regulations actually raises a few very critical questions. For instance, even though the secretary general did call for more regulation he seems to have failed to define what he meant by the term "cyber warfare."

At other times you see he refers to cyber security issues and he did not make any distinction between cyber security and cyber warfare. Lines should be drawn and the lack of these demarcating lines blur what constitutes acts of cyber war and what doesn't.

With regard to the secretary general's observation as to the details of cyber warfare not being discussed by committee members and leaders in general, there are those that argue to the contrary.

For instance, acts of cyber warfare have been discussed at other venues and forums. That is why the world leaders and the public in general know that cyber-attacks have occurred and are aware of the dangers they impose.

Preparing for Conflict

The director of UK's Fidelis Cybersecurity Andrew Bushby once commented that one of the dangers of cyber warfare is the fact that you don't need an entire army of hackers and talented computer geniuses to get the job done. Small groups and single individuals can get stage cyber-attacks as well.

However, even though that might be the case a lot of major cyber groups don't work on their own. In fact, the development of cyber weapons will require a huge amount of resources and not to mention a really huge budget.

Is it possible to be prepared for cyber-attacks? The answer is yes. There are things that you can do to keep yourself safe. However, no one can completely say that they are 100% safe from cyber-attacks. In the next chapter of this book we'll go over the cyber weapons that have been created and used in actual cyber warfare. Much later on we will go over the severity of cyber threats and how you can protect yourself from possible incursions.

Chapter 5: Stuxnet and Other Cyber Weaponry

We mentioned Stuxnet in the previous chapter and we described it as the very first cyber weapon ever discovered and used in actual warfare. It is not just an ordinary cyber worm, virus, or malware since it is extremely—emphasis on extremely—sophisticated in its design.

As it was described earlier, Stuxnet is a weapon. It attacks weaknesses in Windows based operating systems using zero day exploits (more on that later). However, just like any other virus one of its goals is to infiltrate a computer system as well as networks and spread.

However, it doesn't stop there. It will not just infect computers. It is designed to cause damaging effects to its targets. If it attacks the computer system in a factory it will cause the equipment to malfunction and wreak havoc which may cause injury and damage to property.

However, Stuxnet was used to attack nuclear reactors as well as nuclear weapons. Well, not the reactors and weaponized nuclear systems directly but only the centrifuges that are used to produce enriched uranium—the main resource needed to produce nuclear weapons.

How Powerful was Stuxnet?

Now, something that is so complex and powerful as Stuxnet could have been weaponized for wreaking global havoc but we know that its functions were delimited by those who created it.

If it was released to ordinary home computers or those in businesses it would have done nothing except to spread to other computers of course. However, if Stuxnet identified that a computer system is part of a uranium enrichment project then it will commence its attacks.

That's how sophisticated it was. Stuxnet will check a computer's PLC (programmable logic controller). What it will be looking for is the manufacturer or a particular model of PLC—it is actually after those that were manufactured by Siemens.

Note that a PLC is how a computer interacts with industrial machinery. In other words, it is how your computer can communicate with heavy duty machines like the ones you can find in construction sites as well as in factories.

That is why it can detect and attack uranium centrifuges first. Stuxnet will alter the programming of a computer's PLC. What happens is that the centrifuge will spin too fast. If the centrifuge spins too fast for too long the process will destroy the equipment.

Now, of course you would think that the programmers of these PLCs and the computers that control the uranium centrifuges would have created counter measures in case the equipment they were using were to malfunction.

This again shows us another bit of sophistication in the design of Stuxnet. After it has infiltrated a PLC and has made the centrifuge spin too fast and out of control, it will send signals to the controlling computer that everything is working just fine. This makes detection of the problem and equipment failure too late. By the time that anyone finds out, all the infected centrifuges are destroyed.

Researchers found out that Stuxnet utilized zero day exploits. In a nutshell a zero day exploit is a piece of computer code that allows it to spread without you or anybody else doing anything. It just spreads at will. You don't have to download a file, you don't have to click a link, or anything.

If your computer is online and is in the path of the spread of a zero day exploit it just gets into your computer system and runs. They call it a zero day exploit because no one knows about the attack except the attacker—there are literally zero days of preparation that you can do to prevent it.

There are no patches released to protect against it. But that is not the only thing that is truly astounding about this cyber weapon. Most of the time only one zero day exploit is employed in a malware or virus. But in the case of Stuxnet it contained four zero day exploits.

The program code that was used to generate it was massive yet when analysts tried to decode it they found out that it had no bugs—even the best designed viruses had bugs—this one didn't have any. It was no less than a programming masterpiece.

Origin of Stuxnet

It is believed that the development of Stuxnet began back in 2005 but was only used and identified five years later in 2010. It was first identified by the infosec community. It is widely believed that Stuxnet was the product of a joint effort between the United States and Israel. Note that Israel is a global leader in the industry of cyber security (more of that later).

Again, no one can point to them directly because there is no evidence that directly links both governments to Stuxnet. Apart from that, there is also the fact that we mentioned earlier that cyber warfare is one that is shrouded in secrecy.

The proverbial word on the street (if there is such a thing in the world of cyber security) is that both the US and Israel nick named the project as Operation Olympic Games. It is said that the project began under the administration of then US president George Bush. Of course the project wasn't completed during his administration so it continued into the Obama administration.

Of course, nothing official has been stated by either government. However there is this video back in 2011 where Gabi Ashkenazi (the head of the Israeli Defense Forces) listed or mentioned Stuxnet as one of the successes that they were able to achieve during his administration.

Again neither government has admitted anything officially.

Who were the engineers who designed Stuxnet? Some say that France, Jordan, and China may also be possible suspects. And it is also suspected that Siemens may also have lent a hand in the creation of Stuxnet. We will never really know.

From the analysis made by other experts we can deduce that they were highly skilled engineers and of course it couldn't have been developed by just one person. There was a team behind the creation of this cyber weapon.

According to one expert (Roel Schouwenberg) from Kaspersky's Lab, that it would take a team of 10 coders around 2 to 3 years to develop something as sophisticated as this. It would have required a lot of money, a lot of time, and a lot of resources to develop something that sophisticated.

You will need to have machines (aka actual uranium centrifuges) or something similar in order to test your cyber weapon to see if it works. You can't just gain access to that kind of equipment. You need to be well funded and well-connected in order to get on that.

Now, there are several other worms and viruses that have the same level of infection capabilities as Stuxnet. There aren't a lot of them on that caliber. Two of those that have the same level of sophistication are Flame and Duqu. However, no one has identified what their specific purpose is.

But what experts can say is that the fact that they have the same distribution capabilities as Stuxnet, it can be assumed that these two cyber worms were also developed by the same team that created Stuxnet. That also means the team that created it is still active.

The Spread of Stuxnet

As we can see both the US and Israeli government were trying to avoid a regional war. The use of Stuxnet was an alternative approach to say Israeli forces bombing the nuclear facility at Natanz that was processing Uranium at the time. As soon as evidence of the effectiveness of Stuxnet was made available (i.e. destroyed pieces of centrifuges) Operation Olympic Games was set in motion.

The target of the operation was the Natanz facility. Note that the place was air gapped. That meant that there were no wireless signals going in or out. There were no internet cables or phone lines either. The facility was literally off the grid.

So, how were able to send the Stuxnet worm into a computer in that facility? It had to be done via a USB thumb drive. That means someone either a secret operative, an undercover agent, a spy, or someone on the inside brought a USB drive and copied the virus/worm into a computer inside the Natanz facility.

However, now this is the big thing—it got out. After it had done its job and the centrifuges in the said facility were destroyed the virus got out. Iran kept having problems with their centrifuges and that was how the agents found out that Stuxnet was already working.

Once on the internet, Stuxnet spread like wildfire. Remember that it was designed to propagate at an aggressive rate. However, it did little to no damage to other computers at all. Remember that it was designed to attack only a specific type of hardware—Siemens PLCs.

It was anti-virus company Symantec who was able to figure out just what Stuxnet was programmed to do. Their director for Security Technology and Response, Liam O'Murchu, even commented that it was the most complex piece of code that they have ever encountered.

They reversed engineered the virus/malware but of course they couldn't reproduce the program source code. But they were able to decipher the target hardware and the type of damage that Stuxnet was designed to do.

Quite frankly, the entire team was given quite a scare when they finally realized that what they have stumbled upon was an actual international cyber espionage operation. In other words they chanced upon an actual cyber weapon. This was a weapon and it was a malware unlike all the rest—it was worlds apart from the other viruses that were produced since then.

And on top of that it was something that was meant to destroy. It was on a totally different level. There was once a video entitled Zero Days by Alex Gibney (a documentarian and is Oscar nominated). It was once available on YouTube which included interviews with Liam O'Murchu and his team about the discovery and unraveling of Stuxnet.

However, the video has since been brought down although you can try to look it up since maybe someone may try to upload it again either on YouTube or some other online streaming service. I don't know how long will this YouTube video will stay online, but it for now only has 32,000 views and it may be taken down any time soon. Of course, you can also rent it on Amazon prime.

Duqu

Duqu is a new worm that was discovered on September 1, 2011 and it is believed to be related to Stuxnet. It is actually a collection of computer malware. This cyber weapon was discovered by the CrySys Lab (Laboratory of Cryptography and

System Security) from the Budapest University of Technology and Economics.

They also wrote a report about it and in that report they called it Duqu. The name Duqu came from the fact that this computer malware creates files that have a "DQ" prefix. This report was used by Symantec to continue the analysis of this cyber threat.

It was Symantec that suggested that Duqu was related to Stuxnet. However, they quickly add that Duqu actually served a different purpose. They even published a rather detailed technical paper on this worm.

Unlike Stuxnet, the main function of Duqu was not to destroy but rather to gather information and data. It is still a cyber-weapon since one of the goals in cyber warfare is to intelligence gathering. However, Duqu captures a computer's system information as well as keystrokes of users. Those are the two ways how it is able to gain passwords and other sensitive data.

Now, what does it do with the data that it has gathered? According to analysis, Duqu uses or stores/transmits this information so as to enable other future attacks. Kaspersky Lab's reported that both Duqu and Stuxnet have the same platform and they have since referred to it as the Tilded because of the names of files that they created that started with a tilde "~". And that's not all—they also confirmed that there are possibly three more variants floating out there.

Researchers also say that Duqu may also have been programmed using an unknown high level programming language but there are those who counter saying that it may have been written using C with a proprietary form of object oriented framework. One thing is for sure, if they found one Duqu there will be more—in fact there are more versions of this cyber weapon.

Flame Malware

Of course the level of sophistication of cyber weaponry will only continue to grow and develop. And that is the case with the Flame malware. So, you think that Stuxnet is already fearsome? Well, guess again. And so it happens in 2012 a new malware that was even more complex comes along.

The discovery of the Flame malware was announced by CrySys Lab, Kaspersky Lab, and the MAHER Center of Iranian National Computer Emergency Response Team (or CERT for short).

Just like Stuxnet, Flame can spread rapidly over a local area network, over the internet, and it can also spread via USB. It is also as aggressive when it spreads its infection. But its data gathering methods is what makes it really surprising.

Flame can detect and report network traffic. It can also collect your keyboard activity, take screenshots, and it can even record audio. That means if you make a Skype call it can record the conversation.

On top of that it can turn your computer into a Bluetooth beacon. When it does that it will also attempt to gather information from other devices around your computer that are also Bluetooth enabled.

If Flame's data gathering capabilities seem to be already fascinating and complex as they already are, there's more. The next question is how can it store all the data that it is able to acquire? The sheer amount of data that it can collect will be massive.

That is another interesting feature of this malware—what it does with all that data. First it stores the data files that it has collected locally on the infected machine. After that it will transmit everything to a command and control server.

And there are several of these servers scattered around the world in unknown locations. Like a faithful deep penetration agent, it will continue to gather information and transmit them and waits for further instructions from the servers that receive the data.

It is estimated that during the day of its launch this malware was able to infect 1,000 computers. The first victims include private individuals, educational institutions, as well as branches of government. The majority of the infections were in the middle east including countries like Egypt, Saudi Arabia, Lebanon, Syria, Sudan, Palestine, Israel, and Iran. And it should also be noted that the huge majority of infect computer system being in Iran.

So, what happened when Flame was discovered?

This malware actually has a kill command. When it was publicly discovered, a kill command was sent to the initial copies of the Flame malware and then what it does is that it automatically deleted all traces of the malware and its file from the host computer. The makers of this cyber weapon didn't want to leave any trace of their technology behind.

The Features of Cyber Weapons

From what we can observe from these three cyber weapons, we can gather their features. First off, cyber weapons can be in the form of a malware, a worm, or any other form of software. It is employed for intelligence gathering, paramilitary activities, and of course for military purposes as well since they can be equipped with capabilities to actually destroy physical infrastructure.

Characteristics of Cyber Weapons

There are several things that are needed before one can create a cyber weapon:

1. You need a lot of funding to create one. That means that the group that makes them should have access to resources to ensure the best quality from the software that is being built.

2. It can be a state funded project or a non-state group but with access to funds and resources, which may mean support from actual governments.

3. It should meet the specific objectives that it was designed for—it is not meant to just randomly corrupt or destroy files. In fact, it actually is designed to target a specific target. When it infects a non-target computer it will do little to no damage at all.

4. It is technology that is growing and developing—which means we will tend to see better and more sophisticated cyber weaponry in the future.

Sponsorship

One of the most critical distinctions between cyber weapons and other viruses and malware is that the group or agent that created it was sponsored. That means the programming team or engineers that were behind its creation aren't the masterminds.

The brains behind the operation are either state or non-state actors. States of course refer to countries that pay for these projects. When we say non-state actors we refer to terrorist groups and other organizations with similar capacities. These aren't your run of mill criminal gang or black hat hacker group.

Objectives of Cyber Weapon Use

A cyber weapon is a tool that performs the actions of spies and soldiers given their very nature, purpose, and objectives. Using them of course is both illegal and can be considered an act of war (well, that is if it was used during a time of peace).

It breaks laws because their use violates the privacy of individuals and it also undermines the sovereignty of the country that it is used upon. It's like dropping a bomb in another country. But only this time it is done on cyber space and not in the real world—yet these cyber weapons can have real as well as physical impacts.

Other objectives of these cyber weapons include the following:

- **Theft** – it is used to collect and gather data such as government, military, and other forms of classified data. It is also used to collect proprietary and private information from businesses and also individuals. That means it can also be used to steal intellectual property as well.

- **Destruction** – as we can see from Stuxnet, these cyber weapons can be used to cause actual damage or even cause physical harm. And in the most extreme possibilities they can be used to harm people and cause either injury or loss of life.

- **Surveillance** – it can be used to monitor people and gather sensitive information like passwords and others bits of critical information.

Now, even though a cyber weapon can spread throughout the web, these tools have specific targets. They have been observed to have a high level of selectivity when they operate. That means it will identify a target before it performs any of its programmed operations. If your computer is not the target system then the cyber weapon will only do minimal actions.

Now, we have only accounted for 3 cyber weapons. We didn't even go into much detail about the other two and only focused the bulk of our discussion on Stuxnet. But make no mistake about it—there are other cyber weapons that have been employed since.

Apart from the first three here are some more other cyber weapons that have either been classified as such by security experts and/or by governments that have encountered them: Wiper (a type of malware), Mirai (a type of malware), and Great Cannon of China (attack tool that performs DDoS).

Chapter 6: Types of Cyber Attacks

We have already described a few of the known cyber-attacks in passing as we went through different details in this book. In this chapter we will go over the most common types of cyber-attacks employed by hackers and other similar groups and individuals.

What is a Cyber Attack?

A cyber-attack is an offensive action. As we have seen in the case of cyber weaponry in the previous chapter it targets specific types of computers, networks, devices, and even machinery. They are used to steal data, alter your files, and destroy information systems as well as physical property.

1. Malware Attack

We have already seen examples of malwares in the previous chapter. Malware is short for malicious software and it refers to any kind of unwanted app or computer program that gets installed on your device or computer system without your express consent.

It can get into your computer or device via legitimate apps or files that have been infected with them. It basically installs itself and then once installed it propagates in your computer and spreads to other computers in your network.

Malware sometimes lurks in your computer by attaching itself on applications that you are using. It can also spread across the internet when you open an internet connection. Note that there are different types of malware.

Here are some of them:

- *Macro Viruses* – macro viruses are the type that infects programs that contain macro commands (you know those combination keystrokes that you can create with a keyboard combination and others). Examles of such programs are Excel and Microsoft Word.

  This type of virus attaches itself to the initialization sequence of that app or program. That means as Microsoft Word or some other app is getting loaded the virus loads itself onto your computer's memory.

  The macro virus will then execute the programmed instructions in it before the app is functional. That means even by the time you start using MS Word, Excel, or whatever it is, the virus is already running on your computer. The virus then spreads throughout your operating system and it also attaches its code to other parts of the system.

- *Ransomware* – We have covered ransomware in greater detail in chapter 2 of this book so we'll just discuss it briefly here. This type of malware blocks you from access and use to your files and other data. And just like holding your information for ransom, it often comes with a threat to either delete or publish your data unless you pay a ransom ergo the name.

The simplest kinds of ransomware can only lock up your files or maybe your entire computer but you can find ways to get it unlocked. You may even use an antivirus program to get rid of this type of malware and regain access to your files.

However do take note that there are more sophisticated types of ransomware out there. There are some that even encrypt your files, which makes file recovery difficult. You need the decryption key to decrypt your files in such as case.

- *Droppers* – droppers are merely programs that are used to install a virus or malware to your computer. They "drop" them off to your device or computer so to speak.

If that is the case, why is it that droppers are not detected by your firewall or even your anti-virus program? Well, here's the deal—the dropper itself doesn't have any malicious code on it. When your anti-virus program scans it the dropper will only look like some other innocent looking program.

Since it is not detected as a kind of virus it usually passes through into your system without any trouble.

Once it is on your computer it will download the complete virus file onto your system.

- *Worms* – unlike viruses, worms do not attach themselves to any host file. These are self-contained programs that can function on their own. They have the ability to propagate within a network and infect any computer system that they come across. The most common way to spread a worm is through email attachments. When you receive an email that has a worm attached to it, the worm will activate and install itself on your computer when you open the attachment.

  It will then search for your contacts in that email address and send copies of itself to each one of them. Other than propagating throughout your contacts worms can also do a lot of other damage.

  For instance they can flood and overload email servers making sending and receiving emails impossible. They can also do other more sophisticated damage as well.

- *Logic Bombs* – you can think of logic bombs as some kind of time bomb or similar to it. Instead of a timer, it will lay dormant in an infected computer system or device until the right condition is achieved like maybe a certain date and time or an event on your computer system like when you reboot or when you install something.

- *Trojans Horse* – a Trojan horse program takes its name from the large wooden horse that was used to bring down Troy. A Trojan is not a virus and is a bit similar to a dropper.

  But unlike droppers or viruses, Trojans do not download anything (like droppers do) and they do not replicate (like viruses do). They already contain the malware hidden inside them ergo the name of this attack.

  It will not replicate itself but will continue to infect the target computer system or device. It will then open what is called a backdoor—usually a high number port on your computer system so that a hacker and then use it to hack into the computer. That is pretty much the same way the Greeks got into Troy and defeated it.

- *Stealth Viruses* – a stealth virus is a special kind of virus. This type of virus is one that will attack the very thing that protects your computer system—your anti-virus program and maybe your firewall too. That is basically how they stay hidden—they modify your virus protection so that it will report to you that everything is A-Okay.

On top of that any file that has been infected will usually increase in file size but the virus will also make it look like there is no increase made. The date and time of that file is also modified so that your operating system will show only the last time when it was modified before the infection took place.

- *Polymorphic Virus* – according to the name of this virus this is the type that changes its appearance time and time again to conceal itself. It does that by changing its decryption. It encrypts itself and then decrypts itself in cycles.

This change is accomplished with the help of a program called a mutation engine. Both the virus and the mutation engine are encrypted and decrypted over and over again so as to avoid detection. However, new anti-virus programs have been developed to locate them even though it may take time.

- *Boot/System Record Infectors* – boot record infectors attack the operating system. The boot record is the first file that your computer will open on your hard drive since it contains instructions on how to boot up your computer.

That is actually a smart move since the boot record infector will already be loaded and running on your computer by the time your operating system becomes fully functional. That's how it bypasses your computer's protection.

- *File Infectors* – file infectors, by their names, infect files—obviously. But they don't attack every other file on your computer. They look for executable programs (i.e. the ones with the ".exe" extension when you look them up on Windows Explorer or via a command prompt). They find these exe files and they either attach themselves to it or they replace that file using its name (i.e. the malware renames itself into the same name as the exe file). So when you run what should have been the app, you instead run the virus/malware.

2. DoS and DDoS

Another type of cyber-attack is the Denial of Service attack (DoS) and its variant the Distributed Denial of Service attack (DDoS). What these two cyber-attacks do is to overload a computer system's resources so much that it is no longer able to provide for other service requests.

An attacker or hacker will usually infect a lot of other machines and devices using malicious software (malware) and then use them use them to send a lot of service requests to a target system—like a website's server computer. In effect the target system is rendered non-functional.

There is no espionage or damage to files that occur. The goal here is to stop the computer system from functioning. Imagine if that would happen to the computers controlling a power grid, air traffic control, or even to a bank's website/server.

Sometimes a DoS and a DDoS attack is only a precursor or a setup for a second attack. Since the target has been immobilized or neutralized, another attack can be launched. Note that there are several types of DoS and DDoS attacks, which include the following:

- *TCP SYN flood attack* – the goal with this type of attack is to flood connection requests to the in process queue, thus exploiting the small TCP buffer space. That means there will be a lot of connection requests but every time the target system replies to those requests the attacking system will not respond.

What happens is that the target system will timeout since it is waiting for the response from those connection requests. Eventually the system that is being targeted will either be rendered unusable or it will crash since the connection queue has been filled up with a huge load which is more than it can handle.

There are two ways that you can prevent a TCP SYN flood attack. The first option is to increase the size of the in-process connection queue, which is usually small. You will then reduce the timeout on all open connections. The second option is to use a firewall to stop SYN packets that are inbound thus your servers have a layer of protection that stops the flood of requests.

- *Smurf Attack* – the goal behind a Smurf attack is to create a large amount of network congestion. This kind of DoS uses ICMP echo requests to overwhelm a network. The target of this type of attack is the network your computers are on – which means your networking equipment (routers etc.) is the target. To protect your routers and other equipment, you should disable any broadcast that is IP-directed.

- *Teardrop Attack* – a teardrop attack will cause a sequential IP packet's fragmentation and also the length offset fields to overlap. What happens is that the system that receives these packets will try to reconstruct them but obviously will fail. As it keeps on doing this the computer system being targeted will crash.

There are patch updates that prevent and resolve teardrop DoS attacks. If you find your computer reporting this then you can just block ports 445 and 139 and also disable SMBv2. After that you can patch your system that protects it from this type of DoS attack.

- *Botnets* – botnets refer to computers and other devices that have been infected by malware and already under the control of a hacker. You often don't know that their malware is already there.

Hackers will use millions of these botnets to overwhelm the processing capabilities and also the bandwidth of a system that they are targeting. It will be hard to detect where all the online traffic is coming from due to its sheer volume and also the fact that the attack is coming from diverse geographic locations. You can mitigate against botnets with the use of black hole filtering and also RFC3704 filtering.

- *Ping of Death* – if you have tried to troubleshoot your internet connection then you or a helpdesk support technician may have guided you on how to use the "ping" command using a command prompt.

A ping will send packets of data to a designated IP address. Each packet is about 32 bytes—normally. But in the case of a ping of death attack, the hacker will ping the target more than the allowed maximum of about 65,535 bytes.

That size a packet is usually not allowed so a hacker will fragment the packets to overcome that obstacle. What happens later on is that the targeted computer will try to reassemble the packets but will fail due to the size of the packet it is working on.

The computer system will then experience a buffer overflow and it will crash. To prevent this, all you need is a firewall that is set to check if IP packets are fragmented and also it should check if it reaches the maximum size.

3. *Phishing Attacks*

Phishing refers to attacks that are aimed at obtaining passwords, logins, and other related information. There are several ways how hackers can obtain your login credentials.

One way is to send you emails that usually look like they come from legit sources like those from social media, banks, newsletters, and other items that you may have subscribed to. The email will usually have links that you will have to click or an attachment that you will have to download. Once you click it or download the attachment malware will be installed on your computer or device.

When the malware is downloaded the hacker can then monitor your keystrokes or access your login details through the apps that you use (e.g. saved passwords on your web browser).

Other phishing attacks incorporate the use of websites that look like they're legit and will require you to enter your login credentials (e.g. username and password). They may report that you need to change your old password to a new one. What happens is that you will have to enter your old/current password and then make up a new one. Of course when you enter your current password they would have got it.

Other than sending you emails a hacker may use social engineering. That is a fancy way of chatting or contacting you through messages etc. and then gaining your trust. After which the hacker will convince you to visit a webpage or download an item (e.g. a free ebook or some other item).

You can prevent phishing attacks by making sure to check if an email is from a legit source. Hover your mouse pointer over any link to see the destination address on the lower side of your browser. Make sure to check email headers—if it isn't from someone you know then don't open the email and don't click anything in it. You can also use a sandbox environment to test the links and attached items in an email.

4. SQL Inject Attack

A SQL inject is usually performed on websites that are driven by a database. With this type of attack a hacker will enter and execute an SQL query via input data. This means that instead of the usual text or login information is entered, SQL code or SQL command is entered.

Doing that will run some predefined commands which will allow the hacker to access information from the database, download proprietary files, recover content, modify data, among other things.

To prevent SQL attacks you can strictly use J2EE and ASP.NET applications, which are less prone to SQL injects. You can also apply leastoprivilege model permissions to the database on your site. There are several other things that you can do to prevent SQL inject attacks.

5. Eavesdropping

An eavesdropping attack is usually done over network traffic. What a hacker does is to intercept any traffic that comes and goes through a computer network. They can gather a lot of information by doing that. They can capture your passwords, usernames, other credentials, credit card numbers, pass keys, and other confidential information.

Note that there are two types of eavesdropping attacks:

1. *Passive Eavesdropping* – with this type of attack a hacker merely waits for transmissions over the network and "listens" to whatever messages may be conveyed back and forth.

2. *Active Eavesdropping* – with this type of attack the hacker disguises himself or passes along as friendly unit or part of the network. He will then send queries to different transmitters of data (e.g. other computers that are part of the network) so that he could get them to send the information or data he needs. This type of eavesdropping is also called scanning or probing.

The best countermeasure against eavesdropping of any kind is to use data encryption. If your files are encrypted and the hacker doesn't know the encryption key then he can't disguise himself (i.e. his computer) as part of the network.

6. Birthday Attack

This type of cyber-attack will require a bit of math to accomplish. This one is classified as a kind of brute force attack where the hacker will try to guess the password or login credentials over and over.

It is a cryptographic attack that takes advantage of the mathematics behind what is known in probability theory as the birthday problem. An example of this is when a teacher tries to find students with the same birthday.

Let's say there are 30 students. If the teacher tries to guess a specific birthday then he will only have a 7.9% success rate which is computed as $1 - (364/365)^{30}$. However, the probability goes higher if he just checks if two students will have the same birthday, up to 70% actually. The probability is computed using the following formula:

$1 - 365!/((365 - n!) * (365^n))$ (substituting n = 70 here)

7. Drive-By Attack

Hackers can infect your computer's browser, which will in turn install a malware. This can happen when you visit a site that is infected by malware placed there by a hacker. It can be a legit site that they hacked into that saves the malware on your browser or they redirect your browser to a malicious site.

Mounting your own defense against these cyber-attacks will require some understanding of the attacks that hackers will try to use. We have outlined only a handful of the many cyber-attacks that unscrupulous people will try to use on you.

Note that there are already measures that have been created to mitigate against the threats mentioned above and others like them. There are also safe practices that you can use to prevent attacks from happening. We will go over some of the best ways to defend yourself in the final chapter of this book.

Chapter 7: Russia's Cyber Warfare

Russia's cyber warfare was once conducted by the agency known as FAPSI or FAGCI (Federal Agency of Government Communications and Information). They were also responsible for government communications as well.

FAGCI was dissolved in March 11, 2003 and was reorganized into the present day Service of Special Communications and Information or Spetssvyaz. This new organization is under the command of the FSO RF or the Federal Protective Service of the Russian Federation.

Russia's Views on Cyber Warfare and Security

It should be noted that Russia views cyber technology quite differently from the rest of the West. The describe cyber warfare with a different perspective and they also employ their cyber tech with a different approach.

It should be noted that Russian officials today believe that their country is already in conflict both with internal and external aggressors. They believe that their country is already being challenged in the realm of information technology.

They view the internet itself as both a threat as well as an opportunity. The very nature of this technology which fosters the free flow of information is no less than threatening to the country's solidarity.

Their military leaders don't use the same terms as their other counterparts in the rest of the world. For instance, they don't use the terms cyber warfare (kibervoyna in Russian) or even the word cyber (kiber in Russian). They usually just classify it all under a bracket umbrella term—information warfare.

This is a rather broad point of reference to work with. That means it is inclusive of a wider spectrum of intelligence gathering. They include the following:

- Information operations

- Psychological operations

- Electronic warfare

- Computer network operations

The Russians also view the struggle in cyber space to be something that is constant and to a certain degree they may also perceive it to be something that is unending. That means that to the Russians, cyber-attacks conducted against and also for them are part of the regular affairs of war. They are not escalatory in nature and absolutely offensive—it's part of the ongoing struggle in their point of view.

Since Russia views cyber warfare as an ongoing struggle both internally and externally, their military has placed a greater emphasis on their cyber capabilities. However, there is a greater emphasis on their offensive capabilities than their cyber defense. They have practiced the use of their cyber offensive capabilities in tandem with regular armed forces. They use their cyber tech as a force enabler—it supports and enhances the capabilities of their regular armed forces.

At the heart of all the cyber activity in Russia, you will find that a lot of them were performed and executed by cyber syndicates as well as hackvitists. Why does Russia employ them for their cyber warfare? Well, they have mobility on their side as well as a certain level of anonymity, which is perfect for espionage—an indispensable trait in the realm of cyber intelligence.

And what is the primary use of these elements? It is intelligence gathering. But they may also e employed for cyber-attacks as well. however, we may expect that Russia will also formalize their ranks and turn away from crowd-sourced cyber talent.

Russia: It is Information Warfare not Cyber Warfare

The Russians prefer to use informatsionnaya voyna or IW for short. They call it information warfare, which is more holistic a concept compared to cyber warfare. In their view, cyber technology is only one way to enable the Russian state to dominate the world's information landscape. It is part of the entire governmental effort and it will be used alongside more traditional weapons and tactics.

In their point of view they would rather employ information warfare measures in order to achieve any objectives that they have set and obtaining a more favorable response from the worldwide community minus any use of military force. This is according to the Military Doctrine of the Russian Federation (2010).

In their perspective the use of information warfare comes first before actual military force is employed. They are to demoralize disorient the enemy first and to ensure that their moves as justified in the eyes of the public.

Cyber tactics and weaponry are only part of that overall scheme. And because information warfare is at the forefront of operations, it is an acceptable tool to be used both in times of peace and also in times of war. So, technically using cyber tools and weapons is not immediately classified as an act of war in the Russian point of view.

A Latecomer in Cyber Warfare

Believe it or not, Russia is actually a latecomer in the field of cyber warfare. Back in the day only the Federal Security Service was the only government agency that is involved in both disinformation campaigns and cyber propaganda. They were the ones implementing the country's cyber surveillance system called SORM.

Change came along in the 1990s when the original FAPSI was disbanded and their teams reorganized into the different coordinated agencies that the country has today. Their activity increased in 2008 when Russia came in conflict with Georgia.

Russia was victorious in the conflict but it also opened their eyes to their own weaknesses especially in the realm of cyber warfare. This prompted a response from their Ministry of Defense to create military reforms including the creation of a branch that will be responsible for conducting information operations.

Their "troops" would include not just hackers and computer science experts. They will incorporate linguists (covering for the deficit in language capabilities), psychological operations operatives, strategic communications, journalists, and of course hackers.

However, the FSB still remains at the forefront when it comes to Russia's information warfare. The proposed military counterpart has had difficulty trying to recruit suitable troops but they are looking to improve their cyber capabilities in the long term. That means they haven't given up on the idea of establishing a military cyber unit.

In spite of the country being a latecomer in the field of cyber warfare, their cyber teams have proven their mettle in the cyber-attacks they conducted in 2007 against Estonia. As stated earlier in chapter 4 of this book, the Russians were quite successful in the very first large scale cyber-attack in the world.

Russia today remains one of the more aggressive actors in the world of cyber warfare. They have been rather systematic in their efforts to look for vulnerabilities in the networks of other countries. The National Cyber Security Centre in the UK is already working with at least 16 other states to counter this effort by the Russians.

Russian Cyber Attack Timeline

The following is a brief timeline gathered by researchers for NBC News and The Independent that shows probable Russian cyber-attacks that have been conducted through the years.

- **April – May 2007:** DDoS attacks on Estonia. The first ever large-scale cyber-attack in history.

- **June 2008:** Russian cyber troops attacked Lithuania, another former member nation in the Baltic. The government outlawed the display and use of Russian symbols. In response, Russian hackers defaced government webpages with the sickle and scythes and also the 5-pointed star, which were soviet symbols.

- **August 2008:** Georgia's internal communications were shut down when Russian hackers attacked their internet. This was one of the first efforts to coordinate military and cyber tactics.

- **January 2009:** Russian hackers shut down two internet service providers in Kyrgyzstan to convince the government to evict a US military base. Kyrgyzstan agreed and they received 2 billion dollars as loans and aid from Russia.

- **April 2009:** Russians shut down a media outlet in Kazakhstan that criticized Russia.

- **August 2009:** Twitter and Facebook were shutdown in Georgia, which Russian hackers say commemorated the Russian invasion anniversary.

- **March 2014:** Russia staged another DDoS attack on Georgia.

- **May 2014:** Ukraine's election commission was shut down.

- **May 2015:** Russian hackers penetrated the German Bundestag's computer network.

- **December 2015:** The systems of a Ukrainian power station were taken over by alleged Russian hackers.

- **June 2015 - November 2016:** Russian hackers stole information from the Democratic Party network and sent them to WikiLeaks. It is believed that the effort was intended to help Donald Trump win the US elections.

- **October 2015:** A failed attempt on Dutch computers to pull out the report on the downing of Malaysian Flight MH17 over Ukraine. The report stated that pro-Russian rebels shot down the passenger airline.

- **January 2016:** it was discovered that Russian hackers were responsible for the attacks on the Finland Foreign Ministry which occurred several years prior.

- **June 2017:** Russia launched cyber-attacks targeting Ukraine's government, energy, and financial sectors.

- **August 2017:** It is believed that medical files were stolen by Russian hackers from the World Anti-Doping Agency.

- **October 24, 2017:** the launch of the BadRabbit ransomware.

- **March 4, 2018:** A Russian double agent by the name of Sergei Skripal and his daughter were poisoned and found unconscious in Wiltshire City.

- **Late March 2018:** failed spearfishing attacks on the UK Foreign Office.

- **October 4, 2018:** the UK accuses Russia's GRU of cyber-attacks that were conducted media, transport networks, financial systems, and political institutions.

Again, it should be noted that a lot of the charges against Russia cannot be confirmed 100% which is the same thing for all other allegations against other countries who are also involved in cyber warfare.

Retired Air Force Colonel Cedric Leighton explains that the motives behind Russia's style of cyber warfare leans more toward influence operations:

"If you look at the Russians, they're primarily interested in influence operations. What you saw in the 2016 election is a classic influence operation, but what's really key about this is that in a classic influence operation, you don't have to physically manipulate anything. What you're doing is you are getting into people's heads."

Chapter 8: China's Cyber Warfare

Every country approaches cyber warfare in different ways and they also have different motivations. In the previous chapter we looked at how Russia approaches the field of cyber war and also its motives for engaging in it. If Russia is more on the control and influence side of it all, China is on a totally different page when it comes to cyber.

Cedric Leighton describes the Chinese cyber war efforts as being centered on economic purposes. In short, they see it as a means for making China as the next economic superpower in the world.

"When it comes to China, their main focus is really an economic focus. They're interested in going after intellectual property and how they can make it themselves. They can do things like go in and copy the plans for a fighter jet. The F-22 and F-35 were both copied by the Chinese.

They're also looking for intellectual property that companies have. They want to know what oil and gas is doing. If an oil and gas company is starting to explore in a certain area of the world and the Chinese national gas company is also interested in that, they will go in and go through computer files of the U.S. company to find out exactly what is happening, what their geologic readings are, what their geological assessments are, and they will use those same assessments to underbid their U.S. competitor."

China's Breed of Cyber War

Even though the motives behind China's cyber war are different from the most of the world, its concepts and terms are very much similar to that of the United States. Nevertheless the Chinese have transformed their approach so that their cyber efforts suit the culture of communist doctrine.

The Chinese have adopted a dominant stance when it comes to information technology. This paradigm shift began after the United States displayed its supremacy and dominance in the very first Gulf War.

They observed that the success and eventual victory of the US during that war was due to its dominance in Information Operations. You can say that the People's Liberation Army of China began to seriously invest in information warfare from that point onward. They see Information Warfare and Information Operations as tools in a systematic arsenal that they can use to defeat their foes.

China's doctrine and policies when it comes to cyber warfare isn't freely available, unlike the United States. However, experts have observed that China is definitely copying heavily from US cyber war doctrine and that the concepts that they espouse are remarkably similar to their US counterparts.

Major General Wang Pufeng who is considered as the father of Chinese Information Warfare, described information warfare as a type of total war—a fusion of firepower, strategy, electronic, intelligence, and information technology. And that pretty much summarizes which direction China is headed when it comes to cyber war.

In Chinese information war doctrine, there are major elements that must exist:

- Operational secrecy

- Psychological warfare

- Military deception

- Electronic warfare

- Substantive destruction

Top 2 Big Spender

Is China serious about its military preparations along with cyber warfare or information warfare? You can bet it is. According to the Stockholm International Peace Research, China is at number two in the list of countries with the biggest military spending for 2018 at 250 billion US dollars. This is according to Trends in World Military Expenditure.

The number one country so far on the high list is none other than the US at 649 billion dollars. These two countries lead the arms race financially since the rest of the top ten don't even hit half their total expenditures:

- Saudi Arabia (67.6 billion)

- India (66.5 billion)

- France (63.8 billion)

- Russia (61.4 billion)

- United Kingdom (50 billion)

- Germany (49.5 billion)

- Japan (46.6 billion)

- South Korea (43.1 billion)

Keeping It Slow and Steady

China may not be as aggressive as other states such as Russia when it comes to its cyber activities. It is taking the long and slow road when it comes to engaging with powerful countries like the United States. According to the FBI's assistant director for counterintelligence, Bill Priestap, China has learned and understands the lessons that the Soviet Union should have learned from the Cold War.

The Chinese understands that economic strength is at the heart of a nation's power. It doesn't matter how powerful your armies are. If your economy is an ailing sick man in the world then you won't last for long.

The Soviet Union was not defeated because America's armies were better. They were defeated because their economy couldn't keep up. The country eventually went bankrupt to a point where they could no longer recover.

John Demers, assistant attorney general, described the Chinese tactic as "rob, replicate, and replace." They rob you of your intellectual property, replicate it, and then replace you as the supplier of that technology.

He cites the case of Nortel's deal with China's Huawei which started back in 2000. Nortel back then was a successful Canadian telecoms company. After 4 years Nortel's IT security discovered that the company has been extensively hacked. However, despite this discovery, Chinese hackers were still able to continue espionage activities for about a decade.

There was no way to link Huawei with the Chinese government sponsored hackers. However, it should be noted that as Nortel's profitability went down, Huawei prospered. In fact, in 2009 Nortel had to file for bankruptcy protection.

Tech Giant Huawei and Cyber Superiority

Does China's tech giant Huawei pose security concerns? The USA they are. In fact, they have already called for other countries to ban the use or having a partnership with the Chinese telecom company since the US regards Huawei a clear and present danger.

Some countries have already heeded the call of the United States such as Japan, Vietnam, New Zealand, and Australia. They have banned Huawei products in their territories. However, it looks like the UK is calling a rain check on that memo.

They are still currently considering partnering with the tech company to help build non-core elements of 5G technology which is already under way. Of course the company will deny any allegations with regard to cyber security. So far the UK doesn't see any real threat in working with Huawei when it comes to developing their internet technology.

The US has already blocked the company's products and then China counters by drafting new cyber security laws that could also block tech firms from the US. US military and intelligence reports say that Huawei's employees including key personnel (not to mention their CEO) has ties and links to China's military.

Three Main Targets

Government and non-government sponsored cyber operatives from China usually have 3 main targets:

1. Critical infrastructure

2. Military

3. People

The people are often the weakest link in a network. You can't expect small businesses and home users to setup a wide variety of cyber protection. However, Chinese hackers are most likely targeting government employees and high caliber businessmen. An example here is that of the Marriott business hacks—they would rather attack people there especially their high ranking officials rather than the average Joe.

Of course the Chinese will be interested in hacking the latest military technology. But they can't break through the level of cyber security that Central Command has already set up today. That is why they resort to hacking military contractors, which is what happened when suspected Chinese hackers stole a ton of data from Navy contractors about project Sea Dragon.

China has not done anything yet about the critical infrastructure in the US—except of course figuring out how the network works. When we say critical infrastructure we refer to the power grid, medical services, military and intelligence services, gas, internet, water facilities, nuclear power, and others.

Needless to say, sometimes a lot of people worry about the possible classic problems of the US with Russia. However, they fail to realize the country's ongoing struggle against China. There is imminent danger and that is also coming from cyber warfare. One key official in the foray admits to the fact that this often keeps them awake at night.

Multiple Cyber Units

The US has the NSA leading the country's cyber warfare and defense efforts along with Cyber Command and 8 other unified commands under the US Department of Defense. The same multi-agency style is also adopted by China.

One of the branches of the People's Liberation Army is PLA Unit 61398. However, this is not the only cyber force or cyber unit serving under China's banner. As you might have guessed they too have multiple cyber groups. An example of which is PLA Unit 61486, which is also suspected of launching a number of cyber-attacks around the world.

China has a vast talent pool that they can draw upon for recruitment purposes. They are one of the most highly populated countries in the world. They can scout for new talent from its population of 1,419,998,303 (population estimate as of June 27, 2019 by UN estimates).

The US and China in the meantime are not ceasing hostilities—at least not in the military sense. A trade war is still underway between the two countries where each side is adding new tariffs to each side's products. Small farmers and other players in the affected industries are the ones getting the brunt of the trade war.

Now, this trade war is a financial and economic matter, right? What has that got to do with cyber warfare? Considering China's information warfare doctrines it has everything to do with it. Policy makers and entrepreneurs should at least be very careful when considering cyber partnerships with the country.

Chapter 9: North Korea's Cyber War

The hermit country that is North Korea is not something to be dismissed when it comes to cyber warfare. They actually have a few advantages. For one thing they are reclusive and rarely reach out to the world in general.

How is that an advantage? In our overly connected world that is an advantage in itself. It is currently highly improbable to send operatives to or even hack into North Korea effectively.

Note that North Korea is one of the countries that have the smallest internet footprints in the world. On top of that, the bulk of the internet access in and out of the country is routed through China and its protective cyber wall.

Scope of Cyber Operations

Only a small minority of people in North Korea have access to the internet. Remember that the majority of their people live in conditions below the poverty line. The internet in this country is of course controlled by the government and their national intranet is called Kwangmyon.

It is connected to domestic businesses, educational institutions, national websites, and it has email service. However, Kwangmyon is largely disconnected from the worldwide web. Note that the country's elite have access to the internet just like you and me however their usage is extremely monitored.

Some place North Korea along with the other states actively engaged in cyber warfare. They believe that the country is at fourth place after Russia, Iran, and China when it comes to being cyber threats to the west. But there are also cyber security experts who say that people are overestimating North Korea's cyber capabilities.

However, North Korean hackers are definitely getting better – one factor could be the fact that they were trained in Chinese universities that specialize in this subject matter and talent is scouted extensively from different parts of the country. Their hackers have boldly attempted hacking anything from Polish banks to the World Bank.

Cyber Organization

We can't really identify all the official North Korean cyber groups because the country's regime is so secretive. Some experts estimate the size of their cyber army to be anywhere from 3,000 to 6,000 highly trained hackers. They are part of the KPA, RGB, and some other organizations in the regime.

Some of their brightest students are sent to Russia while others are sent to China. But they also have universities like the Command Automation University, Kim Chaek University of Technology, and Kim-Il-Sung University.

North Korean Cyber-Attacks

A lot of the cyber-attacks the country organizes are for financial and economic gain. However, the rest of their attacks are either disruptive or destructive in nature. South Korea of course is their most frequent target but their hackers target the rest of the world as well.

Here are some of the notable cyber-attacks that experts suggest are caused by North Korea.

- **WannaCry** – We have covered the WannaCry cyber-attack in detail in a separate section of this book. Experts suspect/suggest North Korea to be behind it.

- **Bangladesh Bank attack** – in February of 2016, South East Asian as well as Bangladesh banks report the theft of about $81 million. Security experts note the similarity in the code used to other attacks that were also linked to North Korea.

- **Sony Pictures hack** – Sony Pictures experienced a cyber-attack on November 24 leading up to the release of their movie The Interview—a comedy where a fictional Kim Jong-un is assassinated.

- **Hacks on South Korean Banks** – a malware called DarkSeoul was able to evade all of South Korea's cyber security. Banks and broadcast networks experienced outages and network disruptions.

Chapter 10: Iran's Cyber War Capabilities

We have covered Operation Olympic Games in several sections of this book and this attack on Iran is a classic case study on cyber warfare and cyber weapons development. Did Iran learn an important lesson from this experience?

The answer is a quick yes. Since 2011 the country has invested a great deal in improving their cyber capabilities. Their test and learn approach is nothing short of relentless. Within the last few years the country has developed cyber warfare capability that rivals the US, Britain, Russia, and China.

One of the documents released in 2013 into the public by Edward Snowden shows how Iran has widely done surveillance work on the United States. According to another document that was also revealed by Snowden we learn that Iran learned its lessons rather quickly and it learned from the best attacks that were launched against her.

Partnership with Other Countries

According to state media from both countries, China and Iran have agreed on working on a united front and work together in the field of cyber security and information technology. They have agreed to create a joint workgroup to counter threats and the pressures that have been placed on both countries.

Iran's Cyber Military

In 2008 it was estimated that the country's Cyber Military to have around 2,400. However, the country also gets a boost in numbers from private individuals and groups since they encourage their country's hackers to openly attack the US, Israel, and other targets. Unlike other countries, Iran seems to support hackers in their nation.

Should we expect cyber-attacks from Iran any time soon? We know that Iran has probed the US extensively. However, it should be noted that probing a country's infrastructure is not equivalent to an imminent attack. It is one thing to probe for targets and another thing to successfully attack.

The cyber-attacks that Iran conducted from 2011-2013 will no longer work since cyber security has already improved. But not all businesses and governments around the world have updated their systems and that means there are still plenty of targets out in the open.

Chapter 11: Israel and Unit 8200

Perhaps there is no other more prestigious (not to mention notorious) cyber group than that of Israel's Unit 8200 (pronounced as eight two hundred). It's a crack tech group that is responsible for both cyber-attack and defense where the country of Israel is concerned. One of the alleged exploits that they were responsible for was the creation and launch of Stuxnet.

A Female Majority Cyber Group

Another significant yet important detail that anyone might have missed is the fact that the majority of the members of Unit 8200 are in fact women. They don't use the traditional recruitment models when they're out to increase their numbers.

It might surprise you what qualities they are looking for. People might think that will prefer to hire some of the best minds in the tech industry. But that is not the case with Unit 8200.

Instead of looking for people with innate coding skills, what they prefer in candidates are traits that go along the lines of problem solving. They also prefer people with great interpersonal skills. Their recruitment and training process is one that actually emphasizes the creation of female leaders among other things.

It should be noted that Unit 8200 is only a branch of the Israeli intelligence section. It serves under the direction of Aman, the Military Intelligence Directorate of the nation of Israel.

One of the other surprising things about Unit 8200 is the fact that their team is primarily composed of young adults with ages ranging from 18 to 21 years old. They are in fact composed of young blood. Yet despite that fact they are still classified or designated as soldiers.

The period of service is very short for each soldier in Unit 8200. Because of the age range of its members and their short service terms the group relies heavily on selecting people who can learn things quickly and adapt to new environments rather rapidly.

When the Israeli government finds youth who show potential, they put them through after school programs. They look for 16 to 18 year old kids who fit their criteria and put them through these programs where they are taught hacking and coding skills among other things.

At this juncture you can say that the screening process for Unit 8200 has already begun for these young men and women. Yes, these after school programs are the feeder programs which screen the possible next batch of recruits.

Is it worth your while to eventually join Unit 8200? Well, think about it. If you check what happens to their alumni, you will find that a lot of them occupy top positions in many international IT companies as well as tech startups. Many of them also get recruited in firms that are based in Silicon Valley.

According to one of the top execs at the Royal United Services Institute, Unit 8200 is one of the top if not the top technology and intelligence agency in the world today. They rival the best in the world including those from other tech groups including the NSA. Their only weakness is that they don't have the numbers when it comes to staff size.

Brief History of Unit 8200

Unit 8200 was formed as early as 1952 in Jaffa. Back then they weren't as sophisticated as they are today. In fact they only had surplus equipment from the United States. The original name of this military unit was the 2nd Intelligence Service Unit.

Its name of course got changed as the years went by. It was known as Unit 848 in 1976. And they were also known as the 515th Intelligence Service Unit. Their base of operations was moved to Glilot junction, which is its current headquarters.

Today Unit 8200 is the largest unit in the entire Israel Defense Force (IDF). Their soldiers number in the thousands. You can say that this is nation of Israel's equivalent of the USA's NSA.

Several divisions within Unit 8200 have also been created. Each division is responsible for tracking and gathering information from different parts of the world. Is there a chance that Israel's crack unit of hackers and computer wizards checking out and monitoring the activity in your country? You can bet it is.

It's Like Straight Out of the Movies

The experience of the recruits to Unit 8200 is a lot like what you see in the movies. High school kids with skills in hacking and computers are tested and recruited to become part of a secret government branch that they couldn't tell anyone—and that is anyone. They can't tell their parents that the after school extra-curricular was actually some sort of training on how to hack actual computers.

Forbes had an article that highlighted one Avishai Abrahami who was recruited into Unit 8200 back in the 90s. His first assignment was to break into the computers of a country that was hostile to Israel.

The first step was to find a way to get into the said computers. Next he was to figure out the encryption code. Finally he had to find a way to compute how much computing power was necessary to decrypt the data that he was going to obtain.

But that wasn't the only challenge. He had to get it done within the day. Such a task would usually take months or even a year. True to his mettle, he did get the job done without any delays. That's a testament to how brilliant he truly was.

A Tradition of Startups and Multimillion Dollar Companies

Of course, there was life after Unit 8200. You may have heard of Avishai Abrahami but not as one of the soldiers serving under that army unit anymore. If you Google his name you will find that he is the co-founder and also the CEO of the popular cloud based hosting and design website Wix.

Abrahami is now 45 years old and he recalls that in his "class" (we don't know exactly what they called them) there were at least 100 people that he knew personally that founded their own startups or are now high ranking officials in their own tech companies.

These former Unit 8200 members founded cyber security companies, telecommunication companies, and other tech startups. Here is a short list of companies that were founded by former members of Unit 8200:

- Radware

- FST Biometrics

- Hyperwise Security

- Check Point Software Technologies

- Imperva

- CyberArk

- NSO

- Palo Alto Networks

- Adallom

- Argus Cyber Security

- Sequoia Capital

- CybeReason

- BioCatch

You may even be familiar with some of the companies in that list. Abrahami also noted that he knew 10 people from his unit that went on to establish businesses that averaged 500 million dollars in market capitalization. Today, Israel is one of the leaders in the field of cyber security.

Edward Snowden Disclosures

Edward Snowden was a computer security consultant and a subcontractor for the Central Intelligence Agency. He is best known as the whistle blower that leaked out documents and information to the media.

The disclosures he revealed included surveillance programs that were run by the NSA. The material he disclosed appeared in The New York Times, The Washington Post, The Guardian, and others.

As a result of his actions his passport was revoked and he was charged with theft of government property as well as violating the Espionage Act of 1917. He now resides in Moscow where he has been given asylum.

One of the documents leaked out by Snowden was published by The Guardian on September 11, 2013. That document revealed how Unit 8200 acquired unfiltered data on citizens of the United States. Apparently it had the full blessing and an agreement with the NSA.

In Friendly and Unfriendly Terms

This is not the first time that both the NSA and Unit 8200 have been working together. They have worked hand in hand in other operations, such as during the development of Stuxnet and other cyber weaponry. In much later incident, Unit 8200 was reported to have hacked into Kaspersky Lab, this was according to a report submitted by The New York Times on October 10, 2017.

However that incident turned out to be a blessing in disguise. While Unit 8200 hacked into their servers they discovered how Russian hackers were searching their computers in real time. They basically caught the Russians red handed. What they discovered that the Russians were searching for American intelligence programs. They then of course reported it warning their US counterparts.

Of course this already obvious evidence that Israel is definitely spying on the United States. Remember that Unit 8200 alumni are at the upper echelons of many cyber security companies as well as telecom companies in the world today. Others have suggested, such as Philip Giraldi (former CIA officer) and James Bamford (best-selling author and researcher) suggest that they are actually threats to national security.

We can understand why Israel is so aggressive with their cyber security and warfare programs. They are a small nation that is surrounded on all sides by enemies. They need to have eyes and ears not only on perceived threats but also threats that may operate on a global scale.

It cannot be denied that the country has produced some of the best minds in the tech industry. They also lead the world in the cyber security industry and for good reasons. They can be expected to cooperate with their allies and we should also expect them to act on their own accord in the name of self-preservation.

Chapter 12: The USA

The USA is at the forefront and we should say at the frontlines when it comes to cyber warfare. The country is also the biggest target in the playing field. Security experts also agree that the computer networks in the USA are vulnerable.

So, what is stopping other countries at launching massive cyber-attacks on the USA? No one wants to engage in full escalated open war with the giant nation. Different countries like Russia, North Korea, Iran, and others have ran a variety of probes but they haven't released huge stacks of cyber weapons.

Why not? Again, anything that is too large a scale of cyber-attack can provoke the USA and may escalate into military warfare. On top of that, the cyber counterstrike that the country can launch is also a deterrent.

National Cyber Strategy

Unlike a lot of other countries, the USA releases at least some of its cyber strategy into the public. Of course since the day Trump signed it into law it has received both praise and criticism.

Note that the USA employs a multiple agency approach when it comes to cyber security and warfare. Different agencies are working together in this effort such as the NSA, FBI, DoD, CIA, Cyber Command, and others. A 2011 cyber strategy document also released by the White House has reserved the right of the US military to use its forces as a response to cyber-attacks. This provides a legal framework to use military force as a response to hacks and other forms of cyber-attacks on the country—again it works as a deterrent.

The US along with its allies is at the top of the heap but the other countries are hot on its heels. Is there a cyber arms race going on? We can guess and suppose that there is given all the threats attacks going on. But we know that America is stepping things up. Private cyber security companies are also part of the game now and they lend a huge helping hand to the country as a whole.

Chapter 13: Cyber Warfare Incidents

There have been cyber warfare incidents that have been analyzed and documented. A lot of them are the more prominent and also publicized incidents. Sometimes the actual states and/or cyber groups can be identified or hinted at and sometimes they can only be deduced.

In this chapter we will go over some of the details of these cyber warfare incidents. We will include which countries or groups were involved (or possibly involved), what attacks were launched, and what the outcomes were if that information is available. We will also include one of the most prominent incidents in history known as Operation Olympic Games among others. We begin with one of the earliest incidents of cyber warfare in the world that occurred alongside actual armed conflict.

Kosovo - Yugoslavia War

- **Yugoslavia and Kosovo Conflict**

The Serb and Albanian populations in Kosovo have long been ethnically divided. That makes the country a rather highly disputed territory. The long term ethnic violence experienced here eventually capitulated in what was to be known as the Kosovo War, which lasted from 1998 to 1999. Note that the Kosovo war is part of the much larger Yugoslav Wars.

The Kosovo War ended with the intervention of NATO. Yugoslavia was forced to withdraw their troops and Kosovo came under the protection of the United Nations. Since some citizens can't take part in open warfare, they decided to resort to cyber warfare.

- **Anti-NATO Campaign**

In July 1998 NATO started conducting air raids. The Serbs who couldn't help out in direct armed conflict felt that they were duty bound to defend their country in any way they can. Thus they resorted to cyber warfare by forming cyber groups to attack NATO cyber properties which included servers, websites, and other forms on online infrastructure that was exposed.

- **Modern Black Hand and the First Cyber Conflict**

The goal was to disrupt or stop NATO operations. There were many hacker groups that were involved but the one that was most successful was known as Modern Black Hand. The first attack Albanian and Kosovo websites targeting the ones that were used to spread propaganda. Some of the websites that they took down included kosova.com, a propaganda site, and zik.com as well as other news portals.

On July 20, a website was shut down by the hosting company itself after it received threats from hackers. They threatened to delete an entire hard drive on the server of the hosting company if they do not take down specified websites.

One of the UCK websites was also defaced. The threat intensified to the point that the hackers claimed to erase one hard drive for every NATO tomahawk missile that was launched.

Another unfortunate incident was that of NATO bombing a Chinese embassy in Belgrade. NATO of course claimed that it was a mistake on their part but that did not stop the Chinese hackers from retaliating. And that is how China got caught up in the war as well. One CNN report said that the US got involved in the Kosovo War and that the country was also targeted by Chinese hackers.

Chinese hackers joined with Russian hackers to continue cyber assaults. One of the first things to go down were NATO mail servers rendering them useless because of a huge dump of emails sent to these servers that also contained malware attachments.

During this war there were back and forth cyber offensives from both sides. NATO and other countries involved also launched their counter campaigns. A ceasefire was reached after 78 days of actual warfare and also cyber warfare. It was said that NATO won the physical war because of their superior combat preparedness but they were pure novices in cyber space.

Since the US was also sucked into this conflict, why didn't they help their allies? One report from The Guardian said that the Pentagon didn't want to join in the cyber war due to the legal implications that such actions might incur. Apart from that, there were those who believed that the Kosovo War also ushered in the very first cyber war since it was the first time that cyber resources were used in actual warfare.

Stuxnet or Operation Olympic Games

- **US and Iran Conflict**

The United States and Iran have no official or even formal relationship with one another. However, the US may have helped to influence the change of the Iran's president back in 1953 allegedly with the help of British intelligence. Since then the country's president was backed by the US. But that only lasted some 26 years.

In 1979 after mass demonstrations with people taking to the streets the country's president vacated the office and an Islamic leader succeeded in the presidency of Iran. As a result of this rather violent transition the new leader seized the US embassy in Tehran and held the officials and employees there hostage.

This of course escalated the situation and has placed both countries either side of the proverbial war table. In 1988 an Iranian plane was shot down by a US warship, which of course made things worse.

The US accused Iran of secretly developing nuclear weapons. There were also accusations that Iran was party to the 9/11 attacks in 2001. However, not everything was a backward step between these two countries. The heads of state of both Iran and the US exchanged phone calls back in 2013, which may have helped patch things up to some degree. Israel was working behind the scenes since they regarded Iran as a threat.

- **Discovery of Iranian Nuclear Weapons Program**

The US discovered that Iran was developing nuclear weapons secretly through a report from an Iranian opposition group back in 2002. They identified a heavy water reactor which is located in Arak and also a uranium enrichment plant in Natanz. The US accused Iran of having a nuclear weapons program and of course Iran denied the accusations.

- **The United Nations Steps In**

From 2006 to 2010, in response to these accusations and the issues raised by the US, the UN ratifies sanctions against Iran following the country's unwillingness to cooperate with the UN nuclear watchdog.

Israel was more than willing to bomb the Natanz facility but the US convinced the country's leaders not to go through with that action. They demonstrated that there was a way to stop or at least slow down the progress of Iran's uranium enrichment activities. It was at this point that a cyber weapon known as Stuxnet was suggested and tested.

A lot of surveillance work was done prior to the launch of this very first cyber weapon. That basically explains why it was known that the Natanz facility used Siemens Step 7 software along with the Windows operating systems that were installed in the factory's computers.

- **Cyber Attack Initiation**

In 2010, Operatives infiltrated the uranium enrichment plant in Natanz and they installed Stuxnet via USB. Remember that the factory itself and the surrounding area were off grid— meaning it wasn't connected to any type of outside network or internet.

Stuxnet did not commence its attacks immediately. It waited for 13 days. This cyber weapon targeted zero day vulnerabilities in these computers that ran Windows based operating systems.

During this phase of the attack Stuxnet replicated itself throughout all of the computers that were inside the facility. After almost two weeks of spreading the Stuxnet turned on by itself and then began to mess with the centrifuges in the uranium enrichment plant.

The goal of this operation was to sabotage the facility. Stuxnet worked and it made the centrifuges spin faster and/or slower thus eventually destroying them. The operators monitoring the factory did not get any warnings that the centrifuges were already malfunctioning, which is one of the functions of the Stuxnet weapon. The effect was that the centrifuges destroyed themselves.

Through Stuxnet the team that launched the attack could monitor how the uranium enrichment facility was operating. In short they were able to spy on the entire industrial system.

- **Obfuscation**

Note that this cyber weapon was able to replicate itself both on Windows computers at the plant as well as on the programmable logic controllers. The next phase of the attack is also interesting.

Stuxnet hid itself and its files by installing drivers and rootkits on the infected Windows computers and PLCs. Because drivers were installed, it was able to manipulate device requests and thus it can modify the routines of the PLCs. This prevented them from shutting down properly thus lending to the destruction of the centrifuges.

Later news broke out that the Natanz facility was experiencing problems with their equipment. They were also ordering large amounts of centrifuges. This confirmed the success of the cyber-attack.

- **Retaliation**

Iran retaliated after discovering that they were targets of a cyber-attack. DDoS attacks were executed on financial websites in the US.

- **Withdrawal of Hostilities**

An agreement was reached where Iran agreed to stop their Uranium enrichment efforts and the sanctions that were imposed against the country were lifted.

Attack on the Ukrainian Power Grid

- **Conflict Between Ukraine and Russia**

Ukraine and Russia share a thousand year history which is more of a tumultuous history. Both countries trace their history from Kievan Rus a Slavic state which existed from 9th to the 13th century.

Ukraine was always under the control of the powers that be in Moscow even before the formation of the Union of Soviet Socialist Republic in 1922. These two countries also have economic ties. Russia actually exports natural gas to Ukraine, which is one of its biggest markets.

There is an estimated 7.5 million ethnic Russians living in Ukraine. Note that more than 46 million people in Ukraine who report that their mother tongue is Russian. That means these two countries are not only historically and economically tied, they also share cultural roots as well. Russians even consider Ukraine a little brother to their country.

So, where did the conflict between these two countries arise? Russian officials want to maintain a control over the region. There are no natural boundaries between Russia and her neighboring countries. The only natural border that they have is on their western frontier which is made up of mountains and rivers.

Traditionally and practically of course, Russia wants to dominate the neighboring countries as a way to manage and control her security. This influence is necessary if you try to put yourself in their shoes. So what is the motive of the Russian attack on Ukraine? Part of the reason is to exercise territorial control.

- **Disputes and Initial Encounters**

Russia began the assault and reconnaissance using spear phishing campaigns. The targets were administrators and IT staff working in power distribution companies in Ukraine. These employees were sent emails with an MS Word document attachment that contained malware in it.

A popup would come up to enable the macros that came with the document that they would download when they clicked on the attachment. The macros are actually a cyber weapon called BlackEnergy3. This actually spread outside of Ukraine as far as the US and Europe.

BlackEnergy3 and its variants opened backdoors to the user's computers which allowed hackers to conduct reconnaissance and map out entire networks. They were able to access Windows Domain Controllers which allowed them to obtain user account information. They even made it through the SCADA networks and then they set things up before launching their actual cyber-attack.

- **Spring 2015—A Patient Setup**

Russian hackers didn't go gung ho on this matter. They carefully set things up taking months to prepare. The goal was to update the firmware of the machines that were used in power plants and that was done in an industrial control setting—something that has never been done before. You can't help but admire the dedication and ingenuity of this attack.

- **December 2015—Attack Launch**

The malicious updates have been completed—all the firmware has been updated. The converters can be taken out which will prevent those monitoring the power plant to send remote commands so that the breakers can close again when a blackout occurred.

It was December 23, 2015, around 3:30 pm, Russian hackers entered the SCADA networks and they disabled the reconfigured UPS systems. They also sent DDoS attacks to call centers so that customers can't contact customer support and report a power outage. And then they opened the breakers, which triggered massive power outages.

They then sent another cyber weapon called KillDisk, which is another kind of malware. All the system files in the initially infected computers in the power stations were overwritten essentially wiping out the hard drive. This malware also overwrites the master boot record thus these computers weren't able to reboot.

- **Withdrawal of Hostilities**

Russian hackers could have done more damage if they wanted to but they didn't. They could have caused more damage to the equipment in the different power plant substations. The wide spread power failure in Ukraine lasted as long as 6 hours. however, the equipment in the control centers took longer to repair. It took officials until April 2016 to restore them to full functionality.

Russia-Georgia War

Georgia and Russia are two countries that have a long and complicated history. Their relationship dates back hundreds of years which include both religious and historical ties. They had a formal alliance back in 1783 which helped them deal with the Persian invasions.

It was then when the Treaty of Georgievsk was signed by the Russian Emperor and Heraclius II of Eastern Georgia. This was the beginning of Georgia's inclusion into the Russian Empire.

In 1918, after more than a century of being part of the Russian Empire, Georgia established its first republic. However, this did not bode well for the Russians. 3 years later in 1921 the Russian Bolsheviks invaded Georgia and the country was made part of the USSR the following year.

Georgia regained its independence in 1991, which of course strained its relations with Russia. Add to that the fact that the country wanted to join NATO and Moscow supporting separatist groups in Georgia, it should be expected that tensions will rise between the two countries.

- **Disputes Between the Two Countries**

On April 20 2008 an unmanned drone was shot down in Abkhazia—a border between the two countries. Georgia accused Russia of shooting down the drone. Of course Russia denied the charge but sends more troops to Abkhazia saying that they were needed to aid the ongoing repairs for the railway system there.

A UN investigation occurred and it concluded that a Russian fighter jet fired a missile that shot down the drone from Georgia in April 21.

- **Reconnaissance Activities**

Early in July of that year Russian cyber groups have been probing the Georgian network which was rather new at the time. Russian chat rooms and other networks discussed the planned attacks and part of the discussion included both actual physical combat as well as cyber-attacks which were to be done in coordination. The first sign of these probes were DDoS attacks on website of Georgia's president.

- **Cyber Assaults**

As it was discussed earlier, Russia's information warfare includes more than just pure cyber assaults. It included DDoS, propaganda campaign, psych ops which were web based, and hacktivism (e.g. defacing websites and attacks on other web properties).

Analysts tracked the activities the RBN and they discovered that all requests to visit Georgian websites were being rerouted to Turkey and Russia and after that the web traffic was blocked effectively. It took a minimum of two weeks to restore web traffic.

- **Cessation of Hostilities**

Russia and Georgia sign a ceasefire agreement in August with the French President Nicolas Sarkozy present at the occasion in order to broker the deal between the two nations.

Operation Cast Lead

Israel and Palestine have centuries-worth of conflict. However, in the late 1980s all the way to the early 1990s the Palestinian Liberation Organization and Israel have begun to negotiate a peace process between both countries.

Forging a peace accord between two rivaling countries wasn't easy and it took them another decade of negotiations before getting any results. Everything culminated in October 1993 when a peace accord was signed in Oslo.

After that the Palestinian National Authority (PNA) was formed and it was followed with the strengthening of security and economic ties with Israel for the next 6 years. In that accord Israel was referred to as an autonomous region.

However, peace wasn't meant to last. The Second Intifada broke out in 2005 and the PNA was split in 2007. During this incident the Hamas and Fatah factions split in violent clashes. The Hamas faction of Palestine took over Gaza Strip. The result of this incident is the total cancellation of all forms of relations between the two countries—well except for some form of limited humanitarian aid.

This would later erupt into cyber warfare with espionage attempts as well as sabotage on both sides. The main assault would then be dubbed as Operation Cast Lead. Cyber operations began in 2008 and culminate in 2012.

- **Israeli Assault on Gaza**

Operation Cast Lead was an Israeli military assault on Gaza Strip on December 27, 2008. This was countered by cyber-attacks from Arabic hackers that targeted both civilian and government websites.

In retaliation the Israeli government threatened to close all connections going in and out of Gaza. This is when cyber groups known as Anonymous and No One entered the scene.

They even gave Israel a stern warning and demanding that the country should not shut down the internet in the territory.

- **Involvement of State and Non-State Hacker Groups**

However, it should be noted that at the time of this conflict these cyber groups didn't have the technical skills and capabilities to carry out their threats. What they resorted to when Israel didn't heed the warning is to dish out small scale and mid-scale cyber-attacks. They didn't have any zero day attacks stock piled on their cyber arsenals unlike how Israel created their sophisticated cyber weapons.

They usually just attacked old vulnerabilities in websites that haven't been patched. They were able to leak credit card information of more than 35,000 people – mostly Jewish civilians. Another cyber group known as Oujda Tech Group penetrated and defaced more than 40 websites—again mostly non-Israeli government sites. However, it should be noted that in this back and forth conflict in cyber warfare both state and non-state hacker groups were involved.

- **Ceasefire Agreement**

Hamas and Israel entered a ceasefire agreement and all attacks both cyber and military were halted after 4 years of conflict. Israel also eased the blockade they made in Gaza Strip.

WannaCry Ransomware Attack

The WannaCry Ransomware attack is a fairly new cyber-attack that was launched on a global scale affecting more than 150 countries worldwide. Attacks actually began before January of 2016 and it continued to spread to different parts of the world until May 2017.

Patches have been created to protect against it. Cyber security experts say that it is still too early at this point to say whether this cyber weapon was launched by any specific state actor. From the heat of its spread and infection and until today WannaCry is regarded as an effective cyber weapon for sabotage.

- **Reconnaissance Efforts**

It is believed that cyber criminals were behind the creation of the WannaCry Ransomware. However, it is also believed that they were also state sponsored as well—that is at least one state that is interested in developing cyber weapons sponsored them. The level of sophistication needed to develop this cyber weapon couldn't be done without a huge amount of funding and support.

The WannaCry Ransomware undergoes a rather lateral movement within an internal network. It also performs reconnaissance actions as it locates files that are shared across networks. Studies also show that it used the NSA's EternalBlue exploit. This exploit was released by the cyber hacking group that went by the name Shadow Brokers.

- **The WannaCry Attack**

After several months of reconnaissance, this ransomware cryptoworm started its attack May 12, 2017 a Friday. This was an attack at an unprecedented scale infecting more than 230,000 computers in more than 150 countries.

The tricky part about this cryptoworm is that it is not directly saved into a computer's hard drive. That makes is one of the ways it evades the checks made by anti-virus software.

- **Countermeasures**

It is believed tha the Shadow Brokers stole the EternalBlue exploit from the NSA. This implicates the agency since they did not inform Microsoft of the exploit that they discovered but instead they used it to create cyber offensives and tools of their own.

Microsoft discovered this vulnerability in their operating systems in March 14, 2017. They then release security bulleting MS17-010 and they released patches for the different operating systems that they were supporting at the time. This included patches for the following OS:

1. Windows Vista

2. Windows 7

3. Windows 8.1

4. Windows 10

5. Windows Server 2008

6. Windows Server 2008 R2

7. Windows Server 2012

8. Windows Server 2016

- **DoublePulsar Backdoor Tool**

The hackers behind the WannaCry attack built quite a sophisticated set of attacks. They first released what is known as the DoublePulsar backdoor in April 14, 2017. It was reported that by April 25, several hundred thousand computers have been infected with the DoublePulsar backdoor.

WannaCry can attack any computer that has been infected by the DoublePulsar backdoor tool, which creates its entry way into a computer system. In case WannaCry detects that a computer system does not have DoublePulsar installed on it then it installs the backdoor tool on that computer system.

- **A Kill Switch was Discovered**

It was first believed that the WannaCry cryptworm was initially spread via email. However that wasn't the case. Instead of email phishing, it actually spread by attacking vulnerable SMB ports.

The first WannaCry attacks started on May 12, 2017 and experts believe that the attacks initiated in Asia due to the evidence that they were able to gather. Within one day it was able to infect more than 230,000 computers.

Security experts of course advised that computer users that fell victim to this cryptoworm not to pay the ransom that were being demanded on the screen—a typical feature of ransomware. However, despite these warnings there were those who did pay the said ransom but there was no guarantee that the decryption key was ever given to any of the victims.

Nevertheless, it has been reported over social media that a total of $130,634.77 has been paid in spite of the advice of security experts. The hackers used three bitcoin wallets to receive payments. The activity of the wallets can be traced, meaning you can find out who sent the money and who received it and where the funds were moved. However, the identities of the people who owned the wallets could never be determined.

A key turning point came when Marcus Hutchins, a researcher, stumbled upon a kill switch that stopped WannaCry from encrypting the infected computer's data. When this malware attacks, it will first check for this kill switch, which is actually domain name that is hardcoded on it.

If the said domain name was registered, then the attack stops and the WannaCry worm won't spread to other computers in the local network or on the internet. Other variants of WannaCry came out in response to this with different kill switches and there was also another variant that had no kill switch.

The discovery of these kill switches slowed the spread of WannaCry. A second and third kill switch web domains were registered by by Matt Suiche on May 14. The hackers who made WannaCry then tried to take down these domains or knock it offline.

It was later discovered that the encryption key was kept in the infected computer's memory. And that led a way for unencrypt the files of an infected computer. The trick is that you should not kill the WannaCry process which would be running on your system.

2016 US Presidential Elections

After 200 years, the US and Russia still has a tumultuous relationship. There are concerns and issues where the two countries agree on and there are other issues where the ideologies part ways and are worlds apart.

During the 2016 presidential elections, it would appear that Russia wanted to proverbially cast its vote against Hillary Clinton and somehow put Donald Trump in the presidential seat.

- **The Assault**

Russian hackers hack into the Democratic National Committee grabbing emails, messages, memos, and other information. One group/agency was identified by the code name Cozy Bear and another group was identified as Fancy Bear.

It was later found out that these groups used PowerShell commands as one of their tools. They actually used PowerShell backdoors to hack into the computers. The information that they were able to gather was later sent to WikiLeaks and they were published to the public on October 7, 2016.

- **Analysis**

It was found out that the attackers (i.e. Cozy Bear) used a program that was coded in Python, which they called SeaDaddy. That was used in conjunction with a PowerShell backdoor that consisted of a single command that ran persistently over a specified time. It was a simple yet powerful way to hack into the DNC computers. In December 5 the attacks on DNC was widely published and the purposes of Russia (assumed) in their attacks were accomplished since they helped to prevent Hillary Clinton from winning the elections that year.

Operation Buckshot Yankee

This incident changed the US government's approach when it comes to cyber security. You can say that it paved the way for the country's military to bolster their efforts when it comes to cyber defense and offense.

- **Commencement of the Incident**

On October 2008 a worm called Agent.btz spreads throughout the computers in US military bases and installations in Afghanistan, Iraq, and other areas as well. It was considered one of the biggest losses in military intelligence by the Pentagon itself.

To neutralize this malware attack the US army launched Operation Buckshot Yankee. They identified that the very first sign of an intrusion came from within a classified computer system with the US army's network. In other words spies have infiltrated the army.

Agent.btz was sending coded messages to the hackers that planted it. It was a sign that the military presence of the USA on foreign soil has attracted intelligence agencies from around the world. The espionage attacks as well as sabotage work began in June 2008 and the cyber conflict ended on October 2010.

- **Reconnaissance and Assault**

The malicious code that was Agent.btz was uploaded in an actual network that was run by US Central Command—that was how high up the spies were able to infiltrate. It was able to spread undetected. It was able to establish control all over several networks and had the potential to transmit data to servers located in foreign territories.

Agent.btz had the ability to open backdoors in infected computers. This backdoor was to be exploited by a control server. However it was also discovered that the remote control server to which Agent.btz was trying to communicate to did not respond.

- **Aftermath**

It took the US military a total of 14 months to remove Agent.btz completely from their systems. This incident prompted the top officials of the army to push for the creation of Cyber Command Control. It took 2 years for the US military and the NSA to trace which thumb drive was used to hack into their systems. It was determined that a laptop in one of the military bases in the middle east was the culprit—all it took was one laptop and one thumb drive to infiltrate the US army network.

Operation Desert Storm

Operation Desert Storm began in January 16, 1991 but the actual war conflict is known in history as the Gulf War. The war itself was a response to Iraq's invasion of Kuwait. The UN coalition of course was a formidable military force. In response to this, hackers that were based in the Netherlands launched their cyber weapon known as the Morris Worm.

The goal was to gain control of ARPAnet servers. But before they could do that they attacked computers from the Department of Energy so they can get a foothold in US networks. This incident is one where non-state and state cyber actors get involved in actual warfare.

- **Reconnaissance Efforts**

The first sign that recon efforts were underway during the Gulf War was when the MILnet hosts were broken into so as to get to the computers in the DoE. The hacks they used back then are considered rudimentary today which included exploiting vulnerability in the VMS as well as password guessing.

- **Information Gathering**

The hackers were able to break into the computers in the Department of Defense in January 16, 1991. They used grep commands in Unix systems as well as other commands to search for files that are related to Operation Desert Storm and also Desert Shield. They searched for troop movements, weapons systems used, and the type of military equipment on the field.

The hackers were able to gain so much information that they filled up their hard drives quickly. They then downloaded the other files to computers in the Bowling Green University and the University of Chicago.

- **Outcome and Aftermath**

The hackers as it would seem were not politically motivated. They actually tried to sell the information they stole to Saddam Hussein but Hussein did not buy the data, which was sold for 1 million dollars. Hussein thought the info was bogus but if he did buy it then that would have been a huge leverage that he could have used to counteract Operation Desert Storm. The biggest damage of this incident was the fiasco that such a big reveal created.

The Deception Program

This was considered as one of the most notorious cyber-attacks during the Cold War. In 1982, CIA agents disrupted the operations of a Siberian pipeline without using any explosive devices.

- **Before the Conflict**

The USA imposed controls on the current pipeline technology at the time. The project leader of the CIA contrived to introduce altered pipeline technology into the hands of the KGB. American companies got involved in the production of the equipment.

Note that at this time Russia didn't have the same computer capabilities as they do now. They did not have the means to automate pipeline operations, which was a loophole that CIA agents thought that they could exploit.

Altered computer chips were sold to the Russians along with defective plans, and flawed gas pipelines. This also allowed them to try using Trojans for the first time as a cyber weapon.

- **Actual Cyber Attack**

It should be noted that the USSR had their natural gas industry as their major contributor to their economy. They supplied this resource to Europe and other parts of the world. The Trojan software that came with equipment that was supplied with the USSR caused the valves, turbines, and pumps to malfunction.

Pipeline explosions occurred which created a significant damage to the entire system. It should also be noted that there were no casualties when all of this took place. However, this was a terrific blow to the Soviet economy, which contributed to the bankruptcy that would occur later on. Some analysts believe that the Cold War ended not in military conflict but because the Soviet economy broke down—something that they were not able to recover from.

Operation Anarchist

The intelligence agencies of the USA and UK have worked together on a number of occasions. In fact they have even put up facilities where their agents can cooperatively work together. Operation Anarchist which was conducted in 1998 is one of those joint operations. This was one of the many documented operations that were leaked into the public by whistle blower Edward Snowden in 2016.

- **Target and Other Middle Eastern Countries**

The main target of Operation Anarchist was Israel along with other Middle Eastern states that were in possession of advanced weapons systems. This included such countries as Syria, Iran, Turkey, and Egypt. Hezbollah was also included in the list of targets.

- **Recon and Information Gathering**

Israel's UAV drone fleet was the main target of this espionage effort. Video transmissions from these drones were intercepted which allowed spies to gauge the military capabilities of these weapons.

They were also able to monitor live operations where F-16 fighter jets were observed during their bombing runs. The Arrow missile testing was also tracked as they were tested for air launch.

Other Cyber Warfare Incidents

The following is a summary of other cyber warfare incidents that have been recorded. Note that there are many others besides the ones documented here.

1. The Tulip Revolution

- Date: 2005 to 2010

- Countries Involved: Russia and Kyrgyzstan

- Conflict: External intervention and sabotage

- Description: Russian hackers disrupted Kyrgyzstan's parliamentary elections. Websites from mainstream media as well as those from different political parties experienced a lot of technical failures.

2. The Jasmine Revolution

- Date: 2010 to 2011

- Countries Involved: Tunisia and web activists

- Conflict: Sabotage and external intervention

- Description: This is the first time in the Arab world where a nation's leader is removed from office via the uprising of its citizens. The action was facilitated by the country's web activists. Social media was used to spread the word about protest activities.

3. DuQu Malware Espionage Tool

- Date: November 2010 to October 2011

- Countries Involved: Iran and Israel

- Conflict: Interstate espionage using spyware and keyloggers

- Description: DuQu was discovered on September 1, 2011 through CrySys Lab in Budapest. It is a sophisticated virus that was suspected to be linked or a product of Israel. It is a programming masterpiece that contains 100 modules with each module capable of performing a specific and separate task. DuQu can perform video, audio, and other forms of surveillance among other things. That wasn't the only remarkable thing about it—the coding of this espionage tool was flawless. There were no loopholes that you can crack.

4. Defacement of India's Eastern Railway Website

- Date: December 2008 to August 2014

- Countries Involved: India and Pakistan

- Conflict: Sabotage

- Description: The defacement of India's eastern railway website marked the beginning of cyber war between the two nations. The relationship of the two countries isn't really peaceful to begin with. And the Whackerz Pakistan Cr3w defacing an Indian website, it created back and forth events of attacks and retaliations. Several other groups soon got involved including the

Pakistan Cyber Army, Zombie KSA, and the Guards of Hindustan.

5. Anthem Attack

- Date: April 2014 to February 2015

- Countries Involved: USA and hackers sponsored by Asian countries

- Conflict: Sabotage and information stealing

- Description: Hackers attack and steal customer information and data from one of the biggest health insurance companies in the USA—Anthem Inc. Health and other related information of 78.8 people were stolen. Recon efforts began in February of 2014 when phishing emails were sent to a computer user in one of Anthem's subsidiaries.

6. Operation Aurora

- Date: Mid 2009 to early 2010

- Countries Involved: USA and China

- Conflict: Sabotage

- Description: This was actually a series of cyber-attacks which were conducted by the Elderwood Group and other cyber hacking groups based in China. These groups have ties with the People's Liberation Army. Even though Google disclosed the attacks in January 2010 the actual cyber-attacks began by mid-2009.

Google reported that the hackers were after the email accounts of Chinese dissidents.

7. Operation Orchard

- Date: 2006 to 2007

- Countries Involved: Syria and Israel

- Conflict: Sabotage

- Description: The NSA intercepted conversations between North Korean and Syrian agents about a nuclear reactor that was being built. The NSA then sent word to Israel's Unit 8200, their military intelligence and cyber group. Unit 8200 hacked files from a senior Syrian government official by planting a Trojan horse while the said official was in London in 2006. Using this cyber weapon they were able to gather a lot of information about the plant including photos, plans, and stages of construction. In September 5 that year Israeli fighter jets were flying low to Syria, destroyed a radar station and dropped bombs at the Al Kabir site destroying the nuclear plant that was being constructed. The matter was dealt with by all parties in secret with no official protests filed before the UN or other governing body.

8. Shamoon Attack

- Date: 2012

- Countries Involved: Saudi Arabia and Iran

- Conflict: Interstate sabotage

- Description: Shamoon is a cyber weapon also known as Disttrack. It targets Microsoft Windows operating systems that are NT kernel based. The actual target of this attack was the state owned Saudi Aramco Corporation. Emails were sent to the employees and one of the IT technicians opened an email with the malicious link. Data was removed from the computers and sent back to the hackers. 35,000 computers were rendered useless and Aramco needed an entire week to restore their operations. Note that Aramco supplies 10% of the world's oil. An attack of this magnitude could have bankrupted a smaller company.

9. Operation Yellowstone 1

- Date: 2013 to 2014

- Countries Involved: USA and Iran

- Conflict: Interstate sabotage

- Description: This attack was also dubbed as the Sands Corp Attack. Sheldon Andelson made a statement in a panel discussion at the Yeshiva University in New York saying that he will put an end to Iran's nuclear ambitions. This statement of course had repercussions. Iranian hackers wiped out ¾ of the company's servers, phone lines were blocked, email service was down, and the technology that ran the casino went to a complete halt. It cost Sands Corp $40 million in repairs.

Chapter 12: Cyber Terrorism

Perhaps one of the most feared aspects of cyber-attacks and cyber warfare is cyber terrorism. It is also a very controversial term and its definition can be as narrow or as wide or vague as the author can deem it to be.

Defining Cyber Terrorism

When we say terrorism, we refer to the unlawful use of intimidation and violence in the pursuit of political agendas and political affairs. There should be a political motive behind it and also that use of terror on people before we can soundly conclude that such a act can be considered as a form of terrorism.

Unfortunately the usual victims of terrorism are the citizens or civilians of a country, kingdom, or territory. Those who have the least force or influence to deal with terrorism usually fall prey to such ominous acts.

When we hear news of terrorist actions here and abroad we are often reminded of the catastrophic injury, pain, suffering, and loss of life that these deeds can inflict. However, combine the word terrorism with "cyber" then we are talking about something else but is also actually related.

Cyber terrorism in this regard is use of cyber technology (i.e. the internet and other related technologies) to commit violent acts. When we say violent acts in cyber warfare terms, it isn't always tantamount to the loss of life or even to bodily injury. However, it should be pointed out that yes, it is still possible for a cyber-terrorist group to inflict terror, pain, injury, and suffering to others through the means of cyber technology.

The Goal behind Cyber Terrorism

There are two different goals behind cyber terrorism and we can say that one of them is also the same goal in cyber warfare in general. One of the goals is to perform violent acts that eventually result in significant bodily harm and loss of life. Again the motive behind this goal is ideological or political in nature.

Of course, not all acts of cyber terrorism are geared toward that. Some acts intimidate and threaten through the means of the internet. For instance, cyber terrorists may disrupt computer networks deliberately on a large scale basis.

They will employ tools that attack personal computers as well as mainframes and servers using programming scripts, hardware methods, malicious software, phishing, viruses, and others.

Some authorities would rather prefer to narrow things down when they define cyber terrorism and its goals. For instance, they would only designate certain cyber-attacks as terrorism deployed by terrorist organizations. Their actions include anything that involves the disruption of information systems. The end result that these anomalous groups are looking for is alarm, panic, and disruption of cyber services.

Of course there are also others who use a broader definition of the term and thus a broader set of goals behind these acts. That is why some authorities and organizations from different parts of the world would include any form of cybercrime as a type of terrorist act on the part of the perpetrators.

Everyone will need to distinguish between cybercrime and cyber terrorism. For the purposes of definition in this book we will subscribe that the former (i.e. cybercrimes) may be perpetrated without the intent on spreading panic and terror.

On the other hand, cyber terrorism may involve acts that can also be interpreted as a form of cybercrime but with a political or idealistic agenda. I think that is the key difference between these two acts.

Is it possible to commit cyber terrorist acts for personal objectives? Absolutely – and that is why we can also consider individuals who may not be part of any terrorist group that can perform acts of cyber terrorism.

The Dispute Continues

There is a lot of considerable effort behind government agencies in the US and around the world to prevent and if possible end the cyber terrorism and cyber-attacks in general. The FBI (Federal Bureau of Investigation) as well as the CIA (Central Intelligence Agency) already has teams who are greatly involved in this effort.

However, as it was pointed out earlier, there is a debate regarding the scope of cyber terrorism. There is definitely an overlap going on where these attacks are concerned. Some groups such as Kaspersky Lab led by their founder Eugene Kaspersky believe that we should be using cyber terrorism since it is according to them a more accurate term instead of just plain old cyber war.

Kaspersky has been quoted to say that:

> *"...with today's attacks, you are clueless about who did it or when they will strike again. It's not cyber-war, but cyber terrorism."*

Another group, the Technolytics Group defines cyber terrorism as follows:

> *"The premeditated use of disruptive activities, or the threat thereof, against computers and/or networks, with the*

intention to cause harm or further social, ideological, religious, political or similar objectives. Or to intimidate any person in furtherance of such objectives."

Again, that is a pretty broad term and that can include any action that may be construed as a type of cyber-attack. That means an attack on an internet business can also be considered as a type of terrorism.

Again, the main distinction here is the motive behind a cyber-attack. If it has any political, ideological, or even religious motive behind the attack then it can be considered an act of cyber terrorism. However, if the attack is purely personal (the perpetrator just wanted to exact revenge or some other personal reason) or maybe economical/financial (e.g. the perpetrator is looking for monetary gain) then the attack is only classified as a cyber-crime and may not necessarily be a kind of cyber warfare.

To put a stamp to that definition, here is how the US homeland security defines cyber terrorism:

"The use of information technology by terrorist groups and individuals to further their agenda. This can include use of information technology to organize and execute attacks against networks, computer systems and telecommunications infrastructures, or for exchanging information or making threats electronically. Examples are hacking into computer systems, introducing viruses to vulnerable networks, web site defacing, Denial-of-service attacks, or terroristic threats made via electronic communication."

Note that there are 3 key features pointed out over and over again in the definitions by different authorities:

1. It seriously interferes with the current network infrastructure already in place.

2. The act is intended to intimidate a nation's government or a sector (or several sectors) of the public.

3. There is the presence of ideological, religious, or political motive.

Levels of Cyber Warfare Capability

There are several levels of cyber warfare capability. These levels have been created by experts to help categorize every cyber group. The categories are the following:

1. Complex Coordinated Group

Cyber warfare groups that belong to this level or category are those that have the capability to conduct coordinated attacks. You can say that this is the top of the echelon on cyber terrorists or cyber warfare groups and organizations. Since they are highly coordinated in their efforts they have the capability to cause a massive amount of destruction.

These coordinated groups may or may not be affiliated with any government. That means some of the terrorist groups may have cells that are involved in this form of terrorism and some groups that are sanctioned by certain governments may resort to cyber terrorism simply because they have the capability to do so.

2. Advanced Structured Groups

Advanced and structured groups don't have the same level of capabilities compared to complex coordinated groups. However, they can make sophisticated attacks on multiple targets. These groups don't work on just a single network or sector of society. They tend to target several sectors and groups.

They also have the capability to create or at least modify basic hacking tools and systems. An organization on this level can perform target analysis, control, and command. Their tools also have rapid learning capabilities.

3. Simple Unstructured

Sporadic groups and singular individuals belong to this category. They have the capability of using just basic hacks to enter systems. They can only target one system or network at a time since they don't have the necessary tools and/or expertise to get things done. They often use tools that were developed by someone else. But some of them may have the capability to alter the tools they use to suit their needs.

Concerns Over Cyber Terrorism

Since the internet has become a huge part of today's modern way of living, concerns over cyber terrorism has of course increased. Cyberspace affords anonymity to those who perpetrate such acts. All the while it would seem that these cyber terrorist groups are free to threaten and even attack citizens, companies, organizations, and even government branches at will.

Many people believe that cyber terrorism is one of the extreme threats to countries today. It should be noted that cyber terrorist attacks have been going on since the late 90s. However, the response of some countries and global organizations may not be consummate to the level of the threat that is being perceived by the general public.

For instance, it is quite notable that the United Nations only has one branch or agency that directly deals with cyber terrorism—the International Telecommunications Union or ITU.

What is the ITU?

The ITU is the agency of the UN that specializes in cyber terrorism. It is based in Geneva, Switzerland. It is also part of the UN Development Group. The ITU has 12 offices all over the world—some are area offices while the rest are regional offices.

ITU is composed of a private-public partnership backed up by intergovernmental agencies. They include 193 member states and they are also supported and manned by more than 800 private and public sector companies.

ITU was formed in May 17, 1865. Obviously they were not created for the purposes of combatting cyber terrorism. Nevertheless, ITU is definitely one of the oldest intergovernmental organizations in the world. The group was merged with other groups as the years went by and it became a specialized agency by the UN in 1947.

A lot of countries around the world have at least 1 government agency that is at the forefront of combatting cyber terrorist groups. In the USA, the United States Strategic Command has been charged by the Department of Defense to combat cyber terrorist groups.

There is a large threat to the cyber infrastructure of the United States. Even the US Air Force has its own counter cyber terrorist group – Air Force Cyber Command. We all know that a lot of the capabilities of the US Air Force are based on an intricate computer system that can be hacked and exposed to attacks. That makes the creation of its own cyber countering group a necessity.

In February 15, 2013 more than 4 million cyber-attacks were apprehended by a Nebraska based consortium. The operation lasted a total of 8 weeks [1]. In that same report it was identified that the cyber terrorist attacks in the US increased by 20% in the year 2011.

NIS Korea is South Korea's government agency that responds to cyber terrorist threats. It should be noted here that South Korea is one of the countries in the world that has the fastest and most advanced cyber architecture. They employ cutting edge technology as well as high speed internet.

That makes it quite surprising that the country's cyber risk score is at a glaring 884 out of 1000. This is according to 2016 Deloitte Asia-Pacific Defense Outlook. It should be no surprise that the 2013 and 2017 cyber-attacks on the country were so successful. Needless to say, the country is stepping up their efforts to curb cyber terrorism on their shores on top of protecting themselves from cyber terrorist attacks sponsored by North Korea.

The existence of the Cyber Blue Team or the Blue Army of China was confirmed back in May of 2011. Back then this elite unit of cyber specialists was composed of about 30 individuals. We don't know just how many members the Blue Army has today.

China claims that the Cyber Blue Team is only tasked with defending the country from cyber-attacks and other cyber threats but they are also suspected of penetrating the internet systems and infrastructures of other governments as well (we'll go over China's efforts and participation in cyber warfare in a separate chapter).

The Internet of Things and Increased Internet Dependence

As the world becomes more dependent on the internet for a lot of aspects of daily life more people believe that the threat of cyber terrorism and cyber warfare is something that can become quite extreme. Some even believe that such attacks can be quite crippling so as to cause another Great Depression.

Some believe that it is the highest possible (supposedly as they assume) to the United States of America. However, natural disasters are still considered generally as the top threat in any country—including the US.

But one thing is certain and it is the current pace of technological advancement is giving a lot of people access to albeit easier access to the illegal things within cyberspace itself. That includes black markets as well as the Dark Web (we'll go over that too in a separate chapter).

On top of that the development of IoT (the Internet of Things) has allowed the merging of the things that are physical with the things cyber. More and more devices are now getting connected to the web.

That includes construction machinery and equipment, your smart phones, light bulbs, traffic lights, CCTV cameras, satellites, your home speakers (e.g. Amazon's Echo devise powered by Alexa), your TV, medical equipment, military aircraft, and even your car is already part of the internet of things. Remember that every single thing that is connected to the internet can become a potential target of cyberwarfare and cyber terrorism.

One article from the New York Times says the following level of threat that we all face from cyber-attacks and cyber terrorism:

"The appeal of digital weapons is similar to that of nuclear capability: it is a way for an outgunned, outfinanced nation to even the playing field. 'These countries are pursuing cyberweapons the same way they are pursuing nuclear weapons,' said James A. Lewis, a computer security expert at the Center for Strategic and International Studies in Washington. 'It's primitive; it's not top of the line, but it's good enough and they are committed to getting it." [2]

Conclusion: Keeping Yourself Safe from Cyber Attacks

There is a lot of public phobia going on when it comes to cyber security, attacks, and warfare. However, as we have shown in the several case studies that have been cited here it should be noted that conducting a cyber-attack is not as simple as it looks.

Hackers do not have the capability of launching a full scale attack at a click of an icon. It requires a lot of sophistication. Remember that there is still a divide between the cyber world and the physical world. One security expert has advised that in today's terms cyber defense still has a huge advantage over cyber offense.

Dealing with Misconceptions

The biggest misconception about cyber-attacks is that they are things that you can't stop and there is no way that you can protect your information and other resources. However, that is not the actual reality.

Well, here's a fact—there are actually millions of cyber-attacks committed each day. There are billions of people connected to the internet and you can be that the number of attempted cyber intrusions is in the millions worldwide.

There is no way to approximate the actual number of malicious operations carried out so it would be futile to actually put a specific number or range. But this is one important point that should help calm our nerves when considering the potential threats—successful cyber-attacks aren't easy.

Sure there are plenty of attacks occurring day to day but many of these attempts are usually just blocked before they can get access to a computer system. That means if you update your computer's system as often as they come then you are relatively safe.

Successful attacks aren't that many compared to the sheer number of cyber-attacks done each day. However the ones that are successful get a lot of media attention. And that is what drives the perception that cyber-attacks are easily conducted.

Main Problems of Offensive Cyber Weapons

There are defensive cyber tools and there are offensive cyber weapons. Cyber weapons face two major problems—obsolescence and perishability. These weapons are perishable (i.e. once they are used they can never be used again).

After a cyber weapon (it may have took them years to make one) has been launched it will do damage of course. But after some time defenses against it are created and thus rendering it useless.

Obsolescence is when a cyber weapon becomes obsolete after some time. Remember that technology changes and sometimes even the best cyber weapons get left behind and become obsolete tools with the next software update.

Keeping Yourself Safe

There is no 100% guarantee that you can keep your devices both at home and in the workplace protected from cyber-attacks. The 2017 WannaCry cyber-attack has demonstrated that fact. However, it should also be noted that as early as March of that year Microsoft was able to distribute an update that protected a lot of computer systems.

All that you had to do was to download and apply the updates. Other than that you should back up your files too. But there are also other things that you can do to keep your devices as safe as you can make it.

Here are some of the things that you can do right now to keep yourself safe:

- Buy and install reliable computer security software (e.g. anti-virus, firewall, anti-spyware, anti-malware, etc.)

- Set devices to update their operating system automatically

- Sign up for managed DNS services (this applies to businesses).

- Use only new generation browsers. Older browsers are more vulnerable.

- Change your passwords regularly

- You should only purchase software from legit sources. Downloading software from ads and free sites are potentially dangerous.

- Do not click email attachments from unknown senders

- Delete messages and invites from social media from people you don't know

- Always update your software

- Create periodic backups (especially in your office)

- Use a firewall

- Do not visit suspicious websites. There are websites that are infected with malware and spyware.

- Perform system scans on your computers daily.

- Require your employees to use strong passwords

- Control the access to your computer equipment in the office. Only office personnel should be able to login and use your company's computers.

- Each employee should have their own individual user accounts

- Limit employee access to data—there should be access tiers

- Limit the authorization to install new software (works both at home and in the office)

- Manage your social media settings

- Talk to your kids about how to keep safe when using the internet

- Use parental controls and monitor your children's internet usage

- If ever you become a victim of a cyber-attack report it immediately to authorities like the FBI, FTC, etc.

- Get your credit reports and place fraud alerts if you do become a victim

- Secure your email and manage your spam email settings

- Use multifactor authentication as much as possible

- Set folder permissions in the office and at home

- Use web gateway security for your business

- Use VPN and other encryption

- Get cyber insurance to protect your business in the event that you become targets of cyber-attacks.

There is a growing demand for cyber security personnel around the world. After the WannaCry attack in 2017 the demand for cyber security has grown six fold. Cyber security is in the upswing and you can manage to keep yourself safe and aware of the current trends in cyber warfare to keep yourself, your business, and your family safe.

Conclusion

Thank you again for downloading this book!

I hope this book was able to help you learn more about cyberbullying and online reputation.

Once again cyberbullying is a serious issue that can lead to serious repercussions. It can result in things that cannot be undone, such as loss of life. It can affect everyone involved, not just the victim and the perpetrator. It can even cause trauma for the witnesses.

As a parent, it is completely understandable for you to want to keep your children protected. When your children suffer, you naturally want to stop their pain as fast as you can. However, there is really no quick fix or formula for emotional and relational issues. In fact, speed may sometimes increase the pain.

The best way to deal with the situation is to sit down with your children and listen to them. Showing them that you are there for them and that you support them all the way can do wonders for their healing. It is actually what most children ask for. It shows your respect for them as well as help the process the events that transpired. It also helps them learn from the situation, become more resilient, and gain back their sense of dignity.

Cyberbullying can indeed take a toll on a person's sense of self-worth. It may take away a child's dignity and self-esteem. It may make them feel worthless, stupid, or incapable of doing anything right. So, you really have to be strong for your children. Act as a good role model. Be a person that they would want to imitate.

It may be tempting to take away computers and phones or ban them from using social networking sites. However, this is not really the correct solution to the problem. As you have learned from this book, the Internet has become an integral part of life. Social media has become a means for companies and schools to stay in touch with applicants as well as screen their online reputation.

Young individuals continue to grow their social literacy as they communicate with other people. Both the learning and socializing processes occur in social media. Interactions can move swiftly between the online and the offline worlds. Removing a service or electronic device does not really remove the interaction. It has to be noted that context is not a service or device. For many young users, context is a social scene or peer group at school.

In addition, social media is merely another place for children and teenagers to hang out. So, banning them from its use can only contribute to their social issues. It can make them feel left out or marginalized. Their peers can avoid them or no longer include them in their activities. They may also unintentionally exclude them because they are not around.

Keep in mind that marginalization is another form of bullying. So, if you do not want your children to experience this, you should allow them to use the Internet and social media. Just do your best to educate them about responsible online usage. You should also monitor their actions, especially if they are very young.

Furthermore, when a social outlet is banned, negative behavior can move somewhere else. Young users can go offline to rebel. Just think of it this way. When you are talking to someone on the phone and you two get into an argument, your issue will not be resolved by hanging up. The issue about cyberbullying will not be resolved by taking away your children's privilege to use social media and the Internet.

Finally, you should keep in mind that what you see in certain gaming sites or social networking sites is not the entire picture. Whatever you see is most likely just the tip of the iceberg. The cyberbully may have been the one who was actually victimized offline and everything that has happened may just be a result of a chain reaction.

As an adult, you have to be more understanding and open-minded about these matters. You have to realize that the young bullies experience pain too. So, you need to take action to stop the pain that everyone's feeling and come up with a lasting and effective solution. You can contact the parents of the bully and the school administrators to discuss the situation and help you out.

Also, greater visibility due to social media does not necessarily mean that cyberbullying is a larger social issue. People can collectively minimize this issue by becoming good role models to their children. You can also encourage other parents, teachers, and adults to take part in civil disclosure. Do not hesitate to contact and encourage public figures too.

If everyone works together to get social and emotional learning into the school system, the students will be able to reduce bullying. They will also be able to improve their emotional and social skills, as well as increase their social and academic success.

The next step is to teach your children what you have learned from this book and help them grow into responsible human beings.

Finally, if you enjoyed this book, then I'd like to ask you for a favor, would you be kind enough to leave a review for this book on Amazon? It'd be greatly appreciated!

If you like this book, please give us a good review for this book on Amazon! If else, send me a message showing where we can improve at fernandoybus.com. We will be happy to care of any problems.

Thank you and good luck!

www.ingramcontent.com/pod-product-compliance
Lightning Source LLC
Chambersburg PA
CBHW031232250726

48655CB00005B/1916